T0065550

LEADERSHIP SECRETS OF A SLUG

DANA G. VENENGA

WESTBOW
P R E S S®
A DIVISION OF THOMAS NELSON
& ZONDERVAN

WestBow Press books may be ordered through booksellers or by contacting:

WestBow Press
A Division of Thomas Nelson & Zondervan
1663 Liberty Drive
Bloomington, IN 47403
www.westbowpress.com
1 (866) 928-1240

ISBN: 978-1-5127-4614-3 (sc)
ISBN: 978-1-5127-4616-7 (hc)
ISBN: 978-1-5127-4615-0 (e)

Library of Congress Control Number: 2016909516

Print information available on the last page.

WestBow Press rev. date: 9/7/2016

Dedicated to
Brianna and Serena—
You are the two finest daughters a father could have.
I'm so proud of you, and I love you both very much.

This book was edited by
Sylvia Hanna (Venenga)
Dale Venenga
William Lunsford
Kevin Belanger
Thank you all for your kindness and wonderful support.

CONTENTS

CHAPTER 1

A "SLUG'S" LIFE

What the what? A slug? Really? Isn't that a slimy, lazy, little worm-like mollusk? How can a slug teach a human being anything about leadership? Well, to be honest, I'm not a real slug, though a few basketball coaches may have thought I moved as slow as a slug over the course of the years I played in high school and college! In fact, I was extremely blessed to serve a twenty-three-year career in the finest air force the world has ever known, the US Air Force. But yes, in some ways I am most definitely a slug! Please let me explain.

I was assigned to Headquarters Air Force, Office of Surgeon General, located in Rosslyn, Virginia, from 2010 to 2012. Rosslyn is about five minutes north of the Pentagon. I commuted back and forth to work from my home in Stafford, Virginia. Stafford is forty-five miles southwest of DC, off of Interstate 95. Rather than battle the roughly sixteen million cars on I-95 (Okay, just a slight exaggeration, but not much!), I chose to "slug." I'll explain more about "slugging" later, but quickly said, it is a form of organized hitchhiking developed to take advantage of the high-occupancy vehicle (HOV) lanes traversing from just north of Stafford, up I-95, and into DC.

My desire in writing this book is to impart a fun-spirited

review of a few of the time-tested and universally accepted traits of leadership as I saw them displayed (and some that I think anyone serious about being a great leader just needs to know) those many long mornings and afternoons I spent as a simple slug. As a bonus, I threw in some additional thoughts I have on leadership after twenty-three years of active duty and a total of over twenty-eight years in a US military uniform. My hope is that anyone who reads this book can see the simple and easy-to-follow actions that can transform them from a mediocre leader into one of finest leaders his or her peers and subordinates will ever know. This book is not an exhaustive concordance on the many subtleties or theories that are intrinsic in the entire study of leadership. It's more of a quick reference primer on the top-leadership attributes. My hope is that you can read this book in two or three days and use it as a reference guide for foundational leadership strategies for the rest of your career and life. I'm taking a lighthearted, albeit sluggish (pun intended) approach in introducing these leadership traits. However, please trust me that there is nothing light or fluffy about these leadership traits; they are foundational. In my opinion, and in the opinions of the acclaimed authors in the references I'll quote, these leadership traits serve as the bedrock leadership characteristics of any person serious about being a superior leader.

If you notice a Christian bent to this book, that's because there is one! As a Christian (a believer in Jesus Christ as the Son of God who lived, died for our sins, and was resurrected on the third day), I find many principles I'll discuss to be closely linked with that of a person who professes a relationship with God through His Son, Jesus Christ. Though, of course, anybody with knowledge of these leadership principles and a desire to implement them into their leadership styles will excel as a strong leader and as a contributing member of society!

Also, you've hopefully noticed by now I try not to take myself too seriously, and you may be wondering what my credentials are for writing a book of leadership insights. That's a fair question. Upon graduation from high school where I was a decent athlete and not very decent scholar, God handed me the world on a platter by allowing me to attend the US Air Force Academy (USAFA) Preparatory School. The air force, the army, navy, and coast guard have associated preparatory schools designed to better prepare high school students, or prior enlisted personnel, for the rigors of a service academy both scholastically and athletically. The schools are approximately ten months to one year in length and are excellent stepping stones for future academy cadets or midshipmen. At matriculation of each of the service academies, a small percentage of "Preppies" meet up with highly qualified high school students and equally highly qualified prior enlisted personnel to form each year's class.

I clearly remember "getting it" one morning after I had been at USAFA Prep for just a few months. I was walking back from an early morning mail check, feeling very good about wearing a sharp uniform and focused on a defined mission of accomplishing my studies and playing basketball. I realized how much I enjoyed the military aspect of the USAFA Prep School and that trying to graduate from the Air Force Academy was going to be my life's mission for the next five years. I fell in love with the idea of serving my country as a professional airman in the US Air Force. I enjoyed the conformity and unity of being on a "team" of military and student professionals. Plus, I was making tremendous friends who would last a lifetime. I was going to school with some of the finest scholar-athletes in the nation. I was blessed beyond reason.

Fortunately, I met the minimum requirements for a "Preppie" to gain admission to the academy itself and began a very unremarkable career as a cadet. I played basketball for part of my fourth-class (freshman) year. I struggled academically (sense a trend?) but excelled militarily. My coaches and I mutually decided (wink, wink) that I should leave the basketball team the second semester of my fourth-class year to concentrate on the heavy class load. Fast-forward four long and difficult years (academically), and I was extremely blessed to graduate in 1991. I chose the Medical Service Corps (MSC) officer career as the MSC is the air force's medical administration career field. While being an MSC is generally not an edge-of-your seat, nonstop life and death decision-making career, it is a very good environment for leading men and women as a young officer and throughout a career. Please let me be very clear; I have not led men and women in combat, though I have led men and women in a combat-support role. I have huge respect and awe for those who have experienced combat and led men and women in combat. I hang on to their every word when I have the opportunity to hear them speak of their experiences, and I love to read of their experiences. During my career, I commanded at the flight, squadron, and deputy group levels in a series of stateside medical treatment facilities (this means that I led or helped lead anywhere from 5 to 250 people at various times). I retired in 2014 as the administrator of one of the largest air force medical centers (1,700 staff members, $110 million budget) on Keesler Air Force Base, Biloxi, Mississippi. Throughout my career, my major focus was on providing solid, Christian-based decision making and very effective leadership to the men and women I was fortunate enough to work with and for. I also wanted to be a great example of a Christian leader. Knowing I wasn't going to knock anybody's socks off with my less than vast intellect, I knew strong leadership and just plain working my tail off (and, of course, God's grace) were the only ways I would have success as a professional air force airman. More important, I wanted to be the best leader I could. I wanted those I led to know their commander had their best interests at heart while we busted our fannies to accomplish the organization's mission.

I love a quote I read from actor and professional wrestler Dwayne "The Rock" Johnson. He said one of the secrets of success he had learned was to "be humble, be hungry, and always be the hardest worker in the room." That's the way I tried to fulfill my duties as a professional airman. Of course, there were days I failed to live fully up to that mantra, but I hope and pray those days were a small minority over the course of my air force career.

It is certainly true that some people are born to be great leaders. They may have been born with a personality that likes to take charge, born with a vision to accomplish a mission requiring people working together to accomplish it, or born with a few physical characteristics that helped (not guaranteed) that they became effective leaders. Conversely, there are people who have the type of personality (egotism and selfishness) that may preclude them from ever becoming very effective leaders. However, I believe the vast majority of us fall in the realm of not necessarily being born great leaders, but through desire, study, experience, and a love of people, we can become very effective leaders and make positive contributions to our chosen profession and the men and women we work with.

James Hunter wrote the book *The Servant: A Simple Story about the True Essence of Leadership* in 1998. I feel it is one of the finest books on leadership ever written. Of course, the philosophy of servant leadership resounds with my conservative, faith-based belief system. Mr. Hunter uses a fictional story with time-tested lessons on leadership beautifully woven into it. Mr. Hunter, through his characters, makes the argument that anyone and everyone has the opportunity to practice leadership when two or more people are gathered together. However, it takes an *active decision* to acquire and apply leadership skills. Mr. Hunter argues that building influence with others, which is the true essence of leadership, requires a tremendous extension of oneself. He furthers defines leadership as, "The skill of influencing people to work enthusiastically toward goals identified as being for the common good."

Mr. Hunter expands on my above-stated philosophy that solid, even inspirational, leadership skills can be learned because they are exactly that—skills. He goes on to state that skills are simply learned or acquired abilities. He states that leadership is a skill set that can be learned and developed by anyone who desires to hone and practice those skills. Also, if leadership is about influencing others, leaders need to know how to develop influence and how to get other people to do the leader's will for the common good of the organization (Hunter, 28–29).

A quote by legendary American writer and self-improvement guru Dale Carnegie is indicative of how I feel about the material and ideas I've used in writing this book: "The ideas I stand for are not my own. I borrowed them from Socrates, I swiped them from Chesterfield, I stole them from Jesus. And if you don't like their ideas, whose would you rather use?"

While I didn't borrow from Socrates and Chesterfield, I definitely borrowed axioms from Jesus Christ and other courageous and transformational leaders. I borrowed from military heroes, business leaders, and everyday men and women. You'll see that I quote fairly extensively from many various sources. I use these passages from other books, often in their entirety, because I don't want to water down the message and the appreciation for their character that one can glean from these leaders.

As I stated, I tend to use a lot of military leaders as my sources; military men and women are people I believe are heroes, and I know of their tremendous sacrifice and the hardships they and their families have willingly traversed. However, please know that I consider firefighters, police officers, teachers, social workers, and pastors/preachers/priests to be exceptional American heroes and skilled leaders also. America would not be the greatest country on the planet without all of these self-sacrificing people!

CHAPTER 2

SLUGS R US

In order to relieve heavy traffic volume during the morning and evening rush hours, HOV lanes that require more than one person per automobile were built in many major American cities to encourage carpooling and greater use of public transport. The first were built in the Washington DC metropolitan area in 1975. The new lanes, and frustration over failures of public-transport systems and high fuel prices, led to the creation in the 1970s of "slugging." Slugging is a form of hitchhiking between strangers that is beneficial to both parties as drivers and passengers are able to use the HOV lane for a quicker trip. While passengers are able to travel for free, or cheaper than via other modes of travel, and HOV drivers sometimes pay no tolls, "Slugs are, above all, motivated by time saved, not money pocketed". Concern for the environment may not be their primary motivation, but it is a nice by-product (Badger, 2011).

The term "slug" (used as both a noun and a verb) came from bus drivers who had to determine if the people waiting at the stop were genuine bus passengers or people wanting a free lift. The bus drivers had to look out for fake coins—or "slugs"—being thrown into the fare-collection box (Clark, 2003).

In practice, slugging involves the creation of free and unofficial ad hoc carpool networks, often with published routes and standardized pick-up and drop-off locations. In the morning, sluggers gather at local businesses and government-run locations—such as park and ride-like facilities, bus stops, and subway stations—with lines of other sluggers. Drivers pull up to the queue for the route they will follow and either display a sign or call out the designated drop-off point they are willing to drive to and how many passengers they can take to a destination in the Washington DC area. The Pentagon—the largest place of employment in the United States with 25,000 workers—is a popular destination. After getting enough riders to fill the car [three for I-95 and two for I-66], the driver departs. In the evening, the routes reverse (Badger, 2011).

Many unofficial rules of etiquette exist, and websites allow sluggers to post warnings about those who break them. Some Washington DC rules are:

- Drivers are not to pick up slugs enroute to, or standing outside the line, a practice referred to as "body snatching."
- A woman is not to be left in the line alone, for her safety.
- No eating, smoking, or putting on makeup while in someone's vehicle.
- The driver has full control of the radio and climate controls.
- No open windows unless the driver approves.
- No money is exchanged or requested, as the driver and Slugs all benefit from slugging.

- Driver and passengers say "Thank you" at the end. (*Etiquette and Rules of Slug Lines*)

In addition to the above rules, it was obvious that slugs shouldn't talk on the cell phone (though slugs sometimes err on this rule); and, of course, if the driver does engage them in conversation, they should never discuss religion or politics!

The rules of slugging and the actual interactions between drivers and slugs always made me think of the iconic "Soup Nazi" *Seinfeld* episodes. A very angry and aggressive-looking owner worked the ordering line and any infraction to the strict and militaristic rules for ordering soup, which included only speaking when spoken to or making a mistake in ordering the soup in a rigid and prescribed structure, resulted in the owner, also known as the Soup Nazi, yelling, "No soup for you!" in a thick Eastern European accent. The would-be customer was forced to leave the restaurant in shame, and worse, without delicious soup!

I imagined a slug making a mistake like touching the radio, rolling down the window, or actually speaking uninvited to the driver and being kicked out of the car somewhere along I-95 with a loud, "No rrrride for you!"

However, despite the strict rules and seemingly unfriendly aspects of slugging, it can be a very pleasant mode of travel. I made several friends in line while waiting and also became friends with several drivers through the years—drivers who weren't too tired or too hurried to talk and learn more about other people. Obviously, as no money is exchanged, it's very beneficial financially for the slug. At the time, I owned a large Dodge Ram pickup with horrible gas mileage. I estimate that between gas cost and parking at the office, I easily saved $500 per month by slugging.

In addition to the economic benefits, the slug also has virtually unlimited time to nap, pray, read, text, listen to music (wearing earbuds), or just plain think in silence about their faith, family, job, or hobbies. However, perhaps because of the dozens and dozens of leadership books I've read and because I consider leadership to be the number-one job of a professional officer in the US military, or maybe standing in the freezing cold one morning I just started to hallucinate, I actually started to see many firm aspects of leadership in the simple practice of slugging. I saw leadership in waiting in the slug line, I saw it in the driver's picking up the slugs, and I saw leadership in the interactions (or lack of them) while actually in transit. I began to see qualities, traits, and characteristics I'd also seen exhibited in the officers, noncommissioned officers, government service civilians, and contractors I'd worked with for the past nineteen years. I saw examples of integrity, patience, courage, humbleness, character, and situational awareness in the slug line as clearly as I could see the incredibly colorful and beautiful fall foliage of northern Virginia. Standing in the slug line is where the first seeds of inspiration for this book began to take root and sprout.

I appreciate a passage in the Bible book of Ecclesiastes as I think about the theory of leadership. Ecclesiastes was written by King Solomon who was King David's son and the King of Israel immediately after David. In chapter 1, Solomon wrote about the futility of life (apart from a relationship with God) when he stated, "That which has been is what will be, that which is done is what will be done. And there is nothing new under the sun. Is there anything of which it may be said, "See, this is new?" It has already been in ancient times before us" (Ecclesiastes 1:9–10 NKJV).

To be very honest, I feel like Solomon when I say there is

nothing new under the sun regarding leadership philosophy
or practice. After all the years of modern history, is there
anything new that can possibly be said about leadership? We
have theories of corporate leadership and theories of military
leadership. Are there possibly any new theories on leadership
still being developed to lead in business or in the military? We
have theories of selfish leadership, and we have theories of selfless leadership. Is there any way possible to still come up with
a newfangled way of thinking about and implementing leadership that we've not thought of yet? I'm going to answer no to
that question. However, creating new ways of helping people
think about and implement the classical philosophies, characteristics, and traits of leadership is definitely a worthwhile
endeavor. Helping you think about leadership in a slightly
different manner is one of my endeavors in writing this book.
I also want you to think about the selfless characteristics of
Christianity and how they relate to selfless leadership. I want
you to know that while it can be very hard work, being a superior leader can become second nature to you and will lead
to a very rewarding life.

CHAPTER 3

INTEGRITY

No discussion about strong leadership could ever truly begin without centering on integrity. Integrity is the benchmark and most fundamental trait a leader can possess. The question is, "Can we maintain our integrity when temptation or peer pressure strongly come upon or against us?" Do we have the strength of character and the integrity to withstand pressure or temptations from your very suave and persuasive superiors, peers in the office, or even that very attractive coworker when it comes to avoiding doing something that you know in your head, heart, and deep down in your gut is wrong?

I saw integrity exhibited in the slug line in several ways. As stated previously, "body snatching" should be avoided. As a reminder, drivers are not to pick up slugs enroute to the line, standing outside the line, or farther back in line. The driver is supposed to wait for his or her turn to get to the front of the line to pick up the slugs who have been waiting the longest time. Often when people worked together, and the driver saw a friend or coworker farther back in the line, he or she would pick him or her up before getting to the front of the line. While this is infuriating to the slugs ahead of the lucky slugs who got picked up early, it is somewhat understandable and probably shouldn't be considered a huge breach of integrity. However, in my opinion, the slugs farther back in line who resisted and turned down being picked up early showed a tremendous amount of integrity. They knew the hallowed rules of slugging and knew they shouldn't be willing participants in a body snatch. In spite of passing up a ride, even on a cold day, the slugs who showed integrity and waited until they got to the front of the line earned endearing respect and gratitude from their fellow slugs!

It is vitally important to understand integrity, and for the purposes of this book, I'll interchange the word "character" with the word "integrity." I found this anecdote about army major Dick Winters, the commander of (E)asy Company in World War II (WWII), whose story was brought to life in the *Band of Brothers* book and movie. Army historian and retired Colonel Cole C. Kingseed became a close friend of Major Winters and recorded many wonderful leadership lessons in his book *Conversations with Major Dick Winters*. Colonel Kingseed says to understand the importance of character in Dick's life, one only has to read a sampling of his wartime correspondence.

Following the Battle of the Bulge [late December 1944 and into 1945], Dick responded to a letter in which DeEtta Almon [friend from his home-town] asked if it was true that soldiers routinely "raise trouble" when they are off duty. Dick replied, "It doesn't mean that everybody raises trouble. Take it or leave it. I didn't, never have, never will, raise trouble while I am in the U.S. Army. Why? First and most important, I've got my own conscience to answer to. Next, my parents, and then I am an officer in the U.S. Army. I am very proud of it and with the rank and position I hold. I wouldn't think of doing anything to bring discredit to my outfit, my paratrooper boots, wings, the airborne patch, or the U.S. Army. Good morale within an outfit is usually reflected by good conduct away from it. That sounds like an idealistic high school kid, I know, but that's how I feel. (Kingseed, 102)

While Major Winters spoke about integrity regarding the aspect of staying out of trouble, he spoke the absolute rock-solid truth when he said that he had his own conscience to answer to. We all need to develop a conscience that knows we always represent something bigger than ourselves. In this case, Major Winters knew he also represented his parents and then the army. He was compelled to act with character and integrity because he represented something he felt was greater than the short-term pleasure of "raising trouble."

As a Christian, I feel compelled to act with integrity and character because I represent Christ who died on the cross with my sins on His shoulders and rose again that I (and all who accept Him as their Savior) can be free from the eternal penalty of sin. I also felt compelled to do the right thing because of the responsibility of representing the air force uniform that I was privileged to wear with character and honor.

When I was in college, we used to recite the quote, "Integrity is doing the right thing, even when no one is watching." C. S. Lewis is credited with that quote, the same gentleman who wrote *The Lion, the Witch, and the Wardrobe*, which was the first volume in *The Chronicles of Narnia* series. Even if you aren't part of a military service or practice a faith in God, you still have a tremendous opportunity to be a leader within your family, your workplace, and among your friends. You can be an outstanding leader by being true to your integrity about doing what's right and having a positive influence on those around you. Colonel Kingseed goes on to say,

Dick's friend Bob Hoffman shares a memory of Winters and the importance of character. States Bob, "I can tell you that he was the same man when the journey of *Band of Brothers* began as he was when his life's journey ended. When Dick initially viewed the transcript of the TV miniseries *Band of Brothers*, he was offended that Damien Lewis, who portrayed him on film, used excessive profanity throughout the series. Dick immediately wrote a letter to Tom Hanks, resigning from the project because, "I don't want these boys and girls thinking it is acceptable using profanity. You know that is not who I am." Hanks issued a tepid apology, but he claimed it was too late in the production cycle to edit the offensive language. Dick held firm and steadfastly countered each of Hank's points of rebuttal. Winters won again and you won't hear a single offensive word from Major Winter's character. (Kingseed, 102)

What an incredible example of character and integrity! Major Winters was willing to pass up any potential fame or monetary reward because he wasn't willing to be portrayed as anything other than who he was. In this example, he was willing to forgo any success from the movie simply because he did not want to appear to condone profanity. He wanted men, women, and children to know that he didn't swear, and it was okay for them to not swear also.

Author Gary Williams writes about another poignant, more recent example of a dedication to integrity. Mr. Williams wrote about American warrior and soldier, US Medal of Honor winner Navy Lieutenant Michael P. Murphy in the book *Seal of Honor: Operation Red Wings and the Life of Lt Michael P. Murphy*. Lieutenant Murphy was the lead Sea, Air, and Land (SEAL) on a mission as part of Operation Red Wings in Afghanistan in June 2005. The operation was designed to capture or kill Mullah Ahmad Shah, one of Osama Bin Laden's top lieutenants. Shah commanded the militia force known as the Mountain Tigers who had an estimated strength of 40 to 150 men (Williams, 130).

The mission called for a four-man SEAL reconnaissance element to find Shah and document his troop strength. Once Shah was found and his troop strength accurately estimated, Lieutenant Murphy's element was to call in a SEAL team to act as a combined assault and blocking reconnaissance unit. The other SEALs on the team were Petty Officer Second Class Matthew Axelson, Petty Officer Second Class Danny Dietz, and Petty Officer Marcus Luttrell [author of *The Lone Survivor*]. Petty Officer Luttrell was also a highly trained medical corpsman. The SEAL team was supposed to surround and neutralize Shah's camp and then perform a combined direct action assault to neutralize the anti-coalition militia throughout the entire Korangel Valley (Williams, 133).

Lieutenant Murphy led the four SEAL element on the operation. Not long after being choppered into the insertion point and beginning their reconnaissance mission, the team encountered three Afghani goatherds consisting of two older men and a teenage boy. The team now had a huge dilemma. If they let the goatherds go free, the goatherds could contact other Afghanis sympathetic to Shah, alerting him of the mission and compromising the entire operation and potentially endanger American lives. Tying them up and taking their phones could still lead to potential mission and operation compromise if someone sympathetic to Shah found them and learned their story, or it may lead to their eventual death if no one found them and they died of dehydration within four to five days. Lastly, the SEALs could just kill the goatherds outright and hide their bodies, thereby silencing any chance of other Afghanis learning of the mission... end of story (Williams, 142).

True to his strong and inclusive leadership style, Lieutenant Murphy talked to the team about their options, trying to come up with a logical convergence of ideas. At least one of the team members had a strong opinion to kill the Afghans and continue on with the mission.

Petty Officer Marcus Luttrell, in his book *Lone Survivor*, summarizes the Afghanistan war's rules of engagement (ROE) and how frustrating and confusing operations within Afghanistan could be.

> Our rules of engagement in Afghanistan spec-
> ified that we could not shoot, kill, or injure un-
> armed civilians. But what about the unarmed
> civilian who was a skilled spy for the illegal
> forces we were trying to remove? What about
> an entire secret army, diverse, fragmented,
> and lethal, creeping through the mountains
> in Afghanistan *pretending* to be civilians?
> What about those guys? How about the inno-
> cent-looking camel drovers making their way
> through the mountain passes with enough high
> explosive strapped to the backs of their beasts
> to blow up Yankee Stadium? How about those
> guys? (Luttrell, 190)

Petty Officer Luttrell also recounts the discussion Lieutenant Murphy had with his team regarding what to do with the three goatherds.

> The question was, What did we do now? They
> were very obviously goatherds, farmers from the
> high country. Or, as it states in the pages of the

Geneva Convention, unarmed civilians. The strictly correct military decision would still be to kill them without further discussion, because we could not know their intentions.

How could we know if they were affiliated with a Taliban militia group or sworn by some tribal blood pact to inform the Taliban leaders of anything suspicious-looking they found in the mountains? And, oh boy, were we suspicious looking.

The hard fact was, if these three Afghan scarecrows ran off to find Sharmack [at the time of writing *Lone Survivor*, Petty Officer Luttrell wasn't allowed to use Mullah Ahmad Shah's real name] and his men, we were going to be in serious trouble, trapped out here on this mountain ridge. The military decision was clear: these guys could not leave there alive. I just stood there, looking at their filthy beards, rough skin, gnarled hands, and hard, angry faces. These guys did not like us. They showed no aggression, but neither did they offer or want the hand of friendship.

Axelson was our resident academic as well as our Trivial Pursuit king. And Mikey [Lieutenant Murphy] asked him what he considered we should do. "I think we should kill them, because we can't let them go," he replied, with the pure, simple logic of the born intellect.

"And you, Danny?"

"I don't really care what we do," he said. "You want me to kill 'em, I'll kill 'em. Just give me the word. I only work here."

"Marcus?"

"Well, until right now I'd assumed killing
'em was our only option. I'd like to hear what
you think, Murph." (Luttrell, 231-232)

In talking about the situation, including logical arguments
on all sides of the decision, the team decided they needed advice from their SEAL leadership. Unfortunately, cell reception
where they were at in the mountains was extremely poor. The
decision was up to them alone.

After even more discussion that not only focused on
each man's interpretation of the ROEs and what the possible
American military and media reaction may be to the team
killing three unarmed, "harmless" civilians and, was there a
clear "right or wrong"? One team member felt very strongly
that killing them was military necessity in carrying out the
orders of military superiors; one team member was indifferent
and didn't give a strong opinion either way. One team member
knew militarily the decision had to be to kill them, but struggled with the idea of killing unarmed civilians. Lieutenant
Murphy, for reasons of both wanting to the do the right thing
for humanity and the potential aftermath from the military
and American media, thought they should let the goatherds
go free. The team voted and decided to let the goatherds go
free (Luttrell, 233-237).

Even though it was an impossibly difficult decision,
Lieutenant Murphy felt killing them was against the ROE
and was contrary to his sense of integrity. He was a trained
American warrior, but he couldn't justify killing who he
thought to be innocent civilians. In what would soon prove
to be a fateful decision, Lieutenant Murphy stood firm in integrity of doing what he felt God, America, and his family

would expect of him. He let the civilian Afghanis go free. Unfortunately, as is the case so often when dealing with indigenous people in countries where the United States has become engaged in an effort to protect Americans and the rest of the world, the goatherds were anti-American. In this case, they were al Qaeda sympathizers and immediately contacted the Shah's force upon being set free (Williams, 142).

About an hour after setting the goatherds free and moving to a more concealed location, the team knew they'd been compromised as they saw eighty to one hundred heavily armed Taliban fighters moving down the mountain, eventually flanking them on two sides. Soon after the team saw the Taliban, an hour's-long fight ensued. Each team member suffered grievous injuries as they tried to alternately fight and retreat down the mountain.

Despite Lieutenant Murphy's severe injuries, he made one more effort to save his team by summoning help. He broke cover and deliberately walked onto open ground in yet another attempt to gain cell reception. He knew the only way to get cell phone reception was to get into the open for reception. As the team leader, he took it upon himself to make contact (Williams, 144).

In order for you to feel the full gravity of Lieutenant Murphy's actions and the depth of his integrity and leadership that day, I'll again directly quote the next two paragraphs.

> Murphy used his encrypted Iridium satellite cell phone and called back to the Operations Center at J-bad [Jalabad, Afghanistan]. Luttrell yelled at Murphy to take cover, but he kept walking and finally made contact. Luttrell described Murphy's actions: "He walked until he was more or less in the center, gunfire all

around him. And he sat on a small rock and began punching in the numbers to HQ. I could hear him talking, 'My men are taking heavy fire... we're getting picked apart. My guys are dying out here... we need help.' Right then he took a bullet straight in the back. He slumped forward, dropped his phone and his rifle, but then he braced himself, grabbed them both, sat upright again, and once more put the phone to his ear. I heard him speak again. 'Roger that, sir. Thank you."

Having completed his call, he knew help was on the way. Luttrell saw Murphy pick up his weapon and flank to his left out of the line of sight. Luttrell then saw Axelson take another round and rushed over to him, but he could do nothing to help without his medical supplies. Axelson was unable to hold his weapon, but despite his mortal wounds, he placed his weapon on a rock and continued to return fire. Luttrell moved to another location and continued to fight on. (Williams, 144)

Petty Officer Luttrell eventually ran/stumbled/fell down the mountain to a more concealed place, and after about thirty minutes, the gunfire diminished, although Petty Officer Luttrell still heard enemy voices all around him. After several more minutes, the voices ceased, and Petty Officer Luttrell was alone. In time, he would learn that he was the only one of the four SEALs to survive the firefight.

Over the next months and years, as navy leadership learned the full extent of Lieutenant Murphy's integrity in holding true to his belief that America stood for freedom and help for the presumed innocent, and his decision to allow the three goat-herds to go free, he was nominated for and ultimately received the nation's highest military honor, the US Congressional Medal of Honor.

In addition to a few anecdotes from the many books I've read about leadership over my lifetime, I want to share a story about integrity that I observed firsthand during my tour as a squadron commander (commanding seventy-five military and civilian medical administrative personnel), previous to being assigned to the Office of the Air Force Surgeon General in 2010. In the air force, squadron commanders work for group commanders who command entire organizations and work for the wing commander. The wing commander is usually a colonel (Officer 6, or O6) or brigadier general (Officer 7, or O7). The superintendent of my squadron, the highest rank-ing enlisted person and most definitely the "glue" and liaison between our enlisted troops and me, was a senior master ser-geant (SMSgt; Enlisted 8, or E8). As evidence of her top-level professionalism and work ethic, this SMSgt was later promoted to the highest enlisted rank, chief master sergeant (CMSgt; Enlisted 9, or E9). My superintendent was "dual-hatted" as the squadron superintendent and the superintendent of the medi-cal logistics flight. She was very busy with both jobs and most definitely excelled in both. The hallmark of a great superinten-dent is being firm, fair, and compassionate to the members of the squadron, especially the enlisted troops. The hallmark of a great logistician is strict adherence to the many regulations and contract statutes that must be followed to a T. All of those skills plus an energetic, cheerful disposition made my superin-tendent an outstanding person and professional in every way. I sincerely trusted her with every major decision we had to make as squadron leadership. We discussed every situation and more often than not, we went with her recommendation.

While my squadron superintendent exhibited integrity in every situation, one situation displayed her unswerving integrity like never before. Also within the medical logistics office was another senior noncommissioned officer (SNCO), though not as senior as my superintendent. My superintendent had known this other SNCO for many years as friends as they had been assigned together at a previous assignment. When the time came for the SNCO's annual Enlisted Performance Report (EPR), it was accomplished, and the SNCO was rated with the highest score in every category. The SNCO was also a very sharp professional who worked hard, did a great job, and was someone who led the younger airmen with skill and compassion. The only way the EPR could have been better, and had a stronger chance of promotion on the next promotion board, would be if the wing commander signed it. Having the wing commander sign the EPR is called a senior rater endorsement and can be requested if the SNCO has accomplished several, although unfortunately unwritten, but widely known requirements. One such requirement was completion of an associate's degree.

Unfortunately, the SNCO was a few classes shy of accomplishing an associate's degree. My superintendent had previously told the person she wouldn't advocate for a senior rater endorsement through me or the group commander. The SNCO made an appointment to come to talk to me about the issue. Of course, as the superintendent and I discussed every squadron personnel situation, we had discussed this particular conflict before the meeting and reviewed the specifics. Even though my superintendent knew her adherence to the known standards could endanger and even end a long-term friendship, she encouraged me to stick with the standard in place for the group and not recommend a senior rater endorsement. Her integrity would not allow her to cut her good friend a break and bend the rules. Rules are rules, and they had to be followed, regardless of unintended negative consequences. We went with her recommendation, and while it was a very difficult decision, it was the right decision. I was very proud of my superintendent for displaying such a tremendous degree of integrity.

As with any SNCO, my superintendent was the fortunate recipient of numerous air force NCO leadership schools and courses. While I know she started her career with a strong internal sense of integrity and character, she also learned more and honed her integrity and convictions at the schools the air force offered. In fact, all branches of the military afford their airmen, soldiers, sailors, and marines with outstanding opportunities for leadership education and career-field education.

As a testament to the professionalism and extreme expertise of the SNCO who did not receive the senior rater endorsement, the SNCO put his nose to the grindstone, finished his associate's degree, and continued a stellar career. In fact, I learned in early 2016 that he had been selected for promotion to CMSgt himself. What a wonderful story of hard work and dedication being rewarded appropriately! He is a great professional airmen and wonderful person; I'm very proud of him also.

What if we were able to display the level of integrity my superintendent displayed in all of our daily interactions with those we work for and with those who work for us? Do we allow a superior to give us too much credit for work that was accomplished by our team? Or are we quick to deflect inappropriate credit and shine the light on those who performed the work or had the bright idea?

One of my favorite leadership axioms is simply this: "Lead

and show integrity at every opportunity, and when required, use words." We've all heard the phrase, "You can talk the talk, but can you walk the walk?" This is a simple way of emphasizing the importance of not only talking about how you would respond or what you would do in a situation, but actually doing it. The real question is, when it comes right down to it and you are faced with the situation, do you respond in the manner you said you would? Do you not only talk the talk but do you walk the walk? Integrity, of course, works the same way. We can all say we are men and women of integrity and character, but when we are behind closed doors and no one is watching, or even when we are publicly faced with a difficult choice or situation, do we respond with integrity, character, and honesty?

Retired air force B-52 navigator, former instructor of philosophy at the US Air Force Academy, and Oxford-educated PhD Jeffrey Zink developed a brilliant way to think about our integrity and what it takes to keep it intact through the seemingly endless onslaught of attacks against it. He uniquely describes the attacks on integrity we all face every day in his book *Hammer-Proof, a Positive Guide to Values-Based Leadership.* Dr. Zink sets the scenario.

> Imagine that you are looking at a concrete post. A good, sturdy post. Well constructed. Maybe 3 1/2 feet high, 6 inches in diameter. The kind you see so often in front of drive up windows or in front of supermarkets.
>
> Now imagine I have been given the job of removing that post. Tough job, but I think I can handle it. Where are my tools? Do I get a jackhammer? No. How about a winch? Or a chain and a bulldozer? Nope.

All I have is a sledgehammer. Twelve-pound head. Good solid-oak handle. A perfect tool. So I get started. I grab that sledgehammer and take a shot at that post. I hit it as absolutely hard as I can. Boom! With very, very little effect. At least on the post. I've recoiled from the shock of the blow. The post suffers maybe one small chunk for all my efforts.

So I take a second shot at the post. With similar results. Another little chunk goes flying off. But I don't quit. I keep slamming that post. And an interesting thing begins to happen. The more I hit it, the weaker the internal structure of the concrete becomes. And each time bigger and bigger chunks go flying off.

Chunk. Chunk. Chunk

And it's not all that long before I'm standing over a pile of concrete dust. Mission accomplished.

So let's connect this to integrity. Our character is just like that concrete post. Strong, sturdy, rigid. But life is full of sledgehammers. Every time we give in to the flow of the Peer Pressure River when we know it's not the right thing to do, every time we succumb to the temptation to go after short-term, egoistic bottom lines when we really know better, we run a serious risk. We risk the hammer.

Chunk. Chunk. Chunk.

It's in all the little things, in those moments when we convince ourselves that "Nobody will ever know," that we run the greatest risk.

Because at least one person will always know. Always. And that's the very person who will never let you forget. You.

Chunk. Chunk. Chunk.

Here's the question: How many shots from the hammer can we take before we're a pile of character dust, blowing in the wind? I don't know the answer to that question, but I don't think we're quite as strong as concrete.

Here's some good news: When I described that concrete post to you, I wasn't completely accurate. The ones in front of drive-up windows aren't plain concrete anymore. Engineers have redesigned them—they are now concrete encased in a steel pipe. These crafty engineers know that concrete protected with steel won't chunk.

Integrity is the ability to resist chunking. It's like a steel pipe protecting your character. The bad news is that you can't put on integrity in one motion. It goes on a teaspoon at a time. Each time you refuse to give into the temptation to chunk, you get stronger, and it gets easier to say "no" the next time.

And there will be a next time. The sledgehammer is relentless. (Zink, 52–55)

This story is an incredible metaphor on how the world, dishonesty, and evil are constantly attacking our integrity, character, and even our souls. The great thing is, as Dr. Zink stated, just as the sledgehammer can take a chunk out of our integrity and character with every smashing blow, we can strengthen our integrity, character, and moral armor with every moral success we have. Every time we resist temptation, even as simple as taking a small stand for honesty and integrity at work, or even simply resisting the urge to gossip in an effort to make ourselves feel more righteous, we should allow ourselves to feel as if we've added a layer of protection to that steel pipe encasement around our concrete post of integrity and character. Eventually, if we cling to perseverance and the "rightness" of our character and mission, we can transform that steel encasement into an almost impenetrable layer of titanium!

In the book *The Leadership Lessons of Jesus*, Bob Briner and Ray Pritchard develop the theory that Jesus Christ was the greatest leader on earth. They develop seventy-five brief chapters, each of which contains a different way Jesus led with integrity, authority, honesty, and insight. Jesus also led with character and many other traits we wish all leaders had and employed. Mr. Briner and Mr. Pritchard say that Jesus taught with authority. They use Mark 1:22 as the source for this statement: "They [the Jewish people and others listening to Jesus preach] were astonished at His teaching because, unlike the scribes [some of the teachers of that era], He was teaching them as one having authority" (Briner and Pritchard, 12).

Jesus, being the Son of God in the flesh when He was on the earth, taught people as one who knew exactly what He was talking about. In being one of the Trinity of the Father God, the Son, and the Holy Spirit, every word Jesus breathed was absolutely authoritative. He wasn't hesitant, didn't have to check his notes, and didn't have to say, "I'll get back with you on that." Jesus was the ultimate leader and the ultimate teacher! Mr. Briner and Mr. Pritchard state that leaders are always teachers. I'll state that ideally yes, leaders should always try to teach, but some may not be as gifted as others. However, as important as it is for the leader and teacher to know what they are talking about, a leader needs to *be* what he or she is talking about. Mr. Briner and Mr. Pritchard state,

> A leader's words, as vitally important as they are, will only go so far and impact so many unless they truly represent the reality in his or her life. A leader's call for commitment, integrity, dedication, and sacrifice will never be honored unless he or she is committed, honest, dedicated, and willing to sacrifice. Effective and enduring leadership calls for both precept and example. (Briner and Pritchard,12–13)

Simply stated, Jesus talked the talk of leadership, integrity, and character. Even better, he more than excelled in walking the walk; you would say He was perfect!

The world is full of examples of people, not just leaders, who acted with extreme integrity in very difficult situations, in addition to Jesus. The great thing is we can *all* act with integrity even if the evil blows of life have weakened it at some point!

Is his book *American Patriot, the Life and Wars of Colonel Bud Day*, author Robert Coram relays the story about the day Lieutenant Commander John McCain (now Senator John McCain from Arizona) became a prisoner of war (POW) at the Hanoi Hilton in Vietnam during the Vietnam War. Colonel Day had been sharing a cell with a roommate, but one day the camp commander came to him and said, "Now you are nothing. We have the crown prince."

The next day the cell door opened, and a wreck of a man was carried inside on a stretcher and dumped onto the floor. He was in worse shape than Day. Both arms were broken. His leg was broken. A shoulder had been smashed by a rifle butt. He had been stabbed with a bayonet. He was the most severely injured of all the American POWs to enter Hoa Lo [Hanoi Hilton]. He was near death" (Coram, 186).

After Colonel Day introduced himself to the new POW, McCain, "With eyes burning bright with fever, the thin, white haired young pilot looked up from his stretcher and told his fellow prisoners his rank and name. The rank was lieutenant commander, U.S. Navy, the name was John McCain."

McCain had been shot down in late October [1967]. Because he would answer no questions, the North Vietnamese initially refused him medical attention. He was about to die when the guards saw a newspaper story that said the son of Admiral John McCain [his father was a Navy four-star admiral] had been shot down. Admiral McCain was about to become the senior military officer in the Pacific Theater, commander of all American forces fighting in Vietnam. Once North Vietnamese officials realized their prisoner was a celebrity, they hospitalized him, performed surgery, and gave him medications. A constant stream of high-ranking North Vietnamese officers visited him in the hospital. (Coram, 186)

As a long-time senator, John McCain is known for being somewhat of a maverick politician, speaking his own mind and not afraid of ruffling the feathers of other politicians, both Republican and Democrat. He recounts the experience of being offered an early release to go home from the Vietnam prison in his book with Mark Salter, *Faith of My Fathers*.

> For months I had received conspicuously lenient treatment. By the time Bud [Colonel Day] and I were separated, I was able to walk for short distances, and the Vietnamese decided I was fit enough to withstand interrogations, or "quizzes" as the POWs called them. The Vietnamese had caught me communicating several times, and I was forever displaying a "bad attitude" toward my guards. During this period, I possessed the camp record for being caught the most times in the act of communicating, yet the Vietnamese often only punished my offenses with threats. Sometimes they withheld my daily cigarette ration or my bathing privileges, a punishment that served to make me even surlier toward my guards. Once in a while they would cuff me around, but not often, and they never seriously hurt me.
>
> In my first return to the interrogation room after being left alone for many weeks, Soft Soap [the POWs often made up nick-names for the guards] had asked me if I would like to go home. I had replied that I would not go home out of turn [with previous U.S. forces captured]. To this, and with uncharacteristic churlishness,

Soft Soap had said, "You are all war criminals and will never go home."

After I went back to my cell, I relayed Soft Soap's offer up the communication chain to Hervey Stockman, an Air Force colonel who was our senior ranking officer (SRO) at the time. Offers of early release were fairly common practice at the time, and we regarded them as nothing more than psychological torture. So neither the SRO nor I took Soft Soap's inquiry very seriously.

Sometime in the middle of June 1968, I was summoned to an interview with the Cat [a senior camp officer]. His interpreter was an English-speaking officer we called "the Rabbit," an experienced torturer who enjoyed his work. I had been brought to the large reception room in the Big House, the room they often brought visiting peace delegations to for their clumsily staged propaganda displays. The room was furnished with upholstered chairs, a sofa, and a glass coffee table supported by two decorative ceramic elephants. An inviting spread of tea, cookies, and cigarettes had been laid out on the table.

The Cat began telling me about how he had run the prison camps during the French Indochina War, and how he had given a couple of prisoners their liberty. He said he had seen the men recently, and they had thanked him for his kindness. He told me Norris Overly [a previous early release prisoner] and the two

Americans released with him had gone home with honor.

After about two hours of circuitous conversation, the Cat asked me if I wanted to go home. I was astonished by the offer and didn't immediately know how to respond. I wasn't in great shape, and was still considerably underweight and miserable with dysentery and heat rash. The prospect of going home to my family was powerfully tempting. But I knew what the Code of Conduct instructed, and I held back from responding, saying I would have to think about it. He told me to go back to my cell and consider his offer very carefully.

The Vietnamese usually required prisoners who were released early to make some statement that indicated their gratitude or at least their desire to be released. They viewed such expressions as assurances that the released prisoner would not denounce his captors once he was back home, and spoil whatever propaganda value his release was intended to serve. Accordingly, they would not force a prisoner to go home.

As soon as I could, I raised Bob Craner and asked for his advice. We talked the offer over and for a while speculated about what I might be asked to provide in exchange for my release. After a considerable time, Bob told me I should go home. I had hoped he would advise me not to take the offer, which would have made my decision easier. But he argued that the seriously injured should be excused from the Code's restrictions on accepting amnesty and should take release if offered. He said I should go home, as my long-term survival in prison was in doubt.

Close confidants though we had been for months, Bob and I had never really seen any more of each other than a couple of brief glimpses when the turnkeys took one or the other of us to the interrogation room or to the showers. Bob had never observed my physical condition and had only reports from other prisoners and my own occasional references to the state of my health upon which to base his judgement about my fitness for prolonged imprisonment. Yet this good man, who revered our Code of Conduct, and who braved the worst adversity with dignity, offered me a rationale to go home, out of turn, while others in at least as bad shape as I was in remained behind.

"You don't know if you can survive this," he argued. "The seriously injured can go home."

"I think I can make it," I replied. "The Vietnamese tell me I won't, but if they really thought that I'm in such bad shape they would have at least sent a doctor around to check on me."

"You can't be sure you're up to this. What do they want from you in return?"

"They didn't say."

"Well, when you go back, just play along with them. See what they want to let you go. If it's not much, take it."

"I don't think I should go down that road. I know and you know what they want, and we won't let it go any further. If I start negotiating with them, it's a slippery slope. [This is a very insightful attitude toward any potential action that would cause a loss of integrity]. They'll tell me they don't want anything, but they'll just wait until the day I'm supposed to go, and then tell me what they want for it. No matter what I agree to, it won't look right."

I wanted to say yes. I badly wanted to go home. I was tired and sick, and despite my bad attitude, I was often afraid. But I couldn't keep from my own counsel the knowledge of how my release would affect my father, and my fellow prisoners. I knew what the Vietnamese hoped to gain from my release.

Although I did not know it at the time, my father would shortly assume command of the war effort as Commander in Chief, Pacific. The Vietnamese intended to hail his arrival with a propaganda spectacle as they released his son in a gesture of "goodwill." I was to be enticed into accepting special treatment in the hope that it would shame the new enemy commander.

Moreover, I knew that every prisoner the Vietnamese tried to break, those who had arrived before me and those who would come after me, would be taunted with the story of how an admiral's son had gone home early, a lucky beneficiary of America's class-conscious society. I knew that my release would add to the suffering of men who were already straining to keep faith with their country. I was injured, but I believed I could survive. I couldn't persuade myself to leave.

Bob still counseled me to take the offer if the Vietnamese were willing to let me go without getting any antiwar propaganda from me. So I spelled out the reasons why I should not do it.

"Look, just letting me go is a propaganda victory for them. I can tell they really want me to do this. I mean, they really want me to go. And if they want something that much it's got to be a bad thing. I can't give them the satisfaction, Bob.

"Second, I would be disloyal to the rest of you. I know why they're doing this—to make every guy here whose father isn't an admiral think the Code is worthless. They'll tell all of you, 'We let McCain go because his father's an admiral. But your father's are not and nobody cares about you.' And I don't want to go home and see my father, and he wouldn't want to see me under those conditions. I've got to say no."

Bob didn't say much after that. He just wished me well, and then we dropped the matter. Several days later, I went to tell the Cat I wouldn't accept his offer.

I sat for some time in the same well-furnished room with the Cat and the Rabbit, exchanging pleasantries and helping myself to their cigarettes. Eventually, again using the Rabbit to interpret, the Cat asked me if I had considered his offer. "I have," I answered.

"What is your answer?"

"No, thank you."

"Why?"

"American prisoners cannot accept parole, or amnesty or special favors. We must be released in the order of our capture, starting with Everett Alvarez"—the first pilot captured in the North.

He then suggested that my physical condition made my long-term survival doubtful. "I think I will make it," I replied. He told me the doctors believed I would not survive without better medical care. His response amused me, and I smiled when I told him I found that hard to believe, since I never saw a doctor except the indifferent Zorba, whose only prescribed treatment for my condition had been exercise and the consumption of my full food ration.

Cat, who evidently did not share my sense of irony, then tried to convince me that I had permission from my Commander in Chief to return home.

"President Johnson has ordered you home."

"Show me the orders."

"President Johnson orders you."

"Show me the orders, and I'll believe you."

He handed me a letter from Carol in which she expressed her regret that I had not been released earlier with Norris and the other two prisoners. It was the kind of thing you expect your wife to say. I didn't believe Carol wanted me to dishonor myself, and the fact that the Vietnamese had kept her letter from me until now angered me, an emotion that usually serves to stiffen my resolve. I was dismissed with an order to reconsider my answer, and returned, holding my wife's letter, to my cell.

During these sessions, the Cat had promised me that I would not be required to make any propaganda statements in return for my release. I had no doubt he was lying. I knew that once I agreed, the Vietnamese would exert enormous pressure on me to record a statement, and I worried that my resolve would dissipate as I faced the imminent prospect of homecoming.

On the morning of the Fourth of July, Soft Soap entered my cell and mentioned that he knew I had received a generous offer to go home. "You will have a nice family reunion, Mac Kane," he suggested.

"Yes," I acknowledged, "but I can't accept it."

A few hours later, I faced a solemn Cat. That morning, the camp loudspeakers broadcast the news that three prisoners had been chosen for early release. The Cat had summoned me to offer me one last chance to accept his offer. This time I was not taken to the large reception room but to an interrogation room. There were no cookies or cigarettes offered. The Rabbit spoke first.

"Our senior officer wants to know your final answer."

"My final answer is no."

In a fit of pique, the Cat snapped the ink pen he had been holding between his hands. Ink splattered on a copy of *International Herald Tribune* lying on the table, opened to a column by Art Buchwald. He stood up, kicked over his chair, and spoke to me in English for the first time.

"They taught you too well, Mac Kane. They taught you too well." he shouted as he abruptly left the room.

Yes, they had.

The Rabbit and I sat there for a few moments staring at each other in silence before he angrily dismissed me.

"Now it will be very bad for you, Mac Kane. Go back to your room."

I did as instructed and awaited the moment when the Rabbit's prediction would come true.

That same day my father assumed command of all U.S. forces in the Pacific. I wouldn't learn of my father's promotion for nearly a year, when two recently captured pilots were brought to the Plantation. A few months after they arrived, one of them managed to get a one-sentence message to me.

"Your father assumed Commander in Chief in the Pacific, July 4, 1968." (McCain and Salter, 232–238)

With his refusal to accept the early release in 1968 based on his display of tremendous integrity, Senator McCain would endure torture, starvation, injury, sickness, and solitary confinement for almost five more years until his release in 1973. Regardless of whether we agree with his political views, Senator McCain's integrity, character, toughness, and grit in this decision mark him as a man of extreme integrity during that situation.

While the stories and experiences I've shared range from the unfathomable life and death decisions made by Lieutenant Michael Murphy and Senator McCain, to the definitely less-exciting but very tough decision of my superintendent at F. E. Warren Air Force Base, they all show what men and women are capable of when they focus on doing what's right and sticking to their internal core beliefs. In fact, my superintendent's dilemma at F. E. Warren is obviously much more representative of what we may face on a daily basis. Do we stifle our conviction of what is right for the immediate issue of maintaining a friendship, looking good for the boss, or saving some money on income taxes by underreporting our income? The beauty of integrity is that we all can have and practice integrity. We just need to ensure we know what is right and hold ourselves accountable to doing what is right. I know acting with integrity in all things can be very difficult. I understand doing what is right can make life hard as we potentially lose friendships or promotions because we refused to compromise our integrity. Trust me… I understand. But in the end, knowing we didn't compromise our integrity will mean a great deal to how we perceive ourselves. You can do it. Learn what is right, and just do it!

CHAPTER 4

COURAGE OVER FEAR

But how does anyone—Green Beret, Navy SEAL, whatever—learn to be that brave? I can't explain it. No one can, we are taught to understand, correctly, that courage is not the absence of fear, but the capacity for action despite our fears.
—Captain John McCain, USN (Ret.),
Why Courage Matters

One of my favorite stories of incredible courage is the biblical story of David and Goliath. Most of us grew up hearing this unbelievable story in church Sunday school or even on a family-friendly cartoon on TV. As you read this story again, or even for the first time, try to put yourself into David's sandals, and imagine what he saw and what he felt. The principal story is taken from the book of 1 Samuel. For historical background, you should know that the Israelites were God's original chosen people. He had loved them and protected them for many years and was in the process of helping them fully occupy the land of Israel that He had promised their forefathers Abraham, Isaac, and Jacob. This is the land that God had often stated, "was flowing with milk and honey," as a way of describing its beauty and natural resources. We pick up the story as the Israelites and the Philistines are preparing for another battle.

> [1]Now the Philistines gathered their armies together to battle, and were gathered at Sochoh, which *belongs* to Judah; they encamped between Sochoh and Azekah, in Ephes Dammim. [2]And Saul and the men of Israel were gathered together, and they encamped in the Valley of Elah, and drew up in battle array against the Philistines. [3]The Philistines stood on a mountain on one side, and Israel stood on a mountain on the other side, with a valley between them.
>
> [4]And a champion went out from the camp of the Philistines, named Goliath, from Gath, whose height *was* six cubits and a span [over 9 feet tall]. [5]*He had* a bronze helmet on his head, and he *was* armed with a coat of mail, and the weight of the coat *was* five thousand shekels [approximately 125 lbs.] of bronze. [6]And *he had* bronze armor on his legs and a bronze javelin between his shoulders. [7]Now the staff of his spear *was* like a weaver's beam, and his iron spearhead *weighed* six hundred shekels [approximately 15 lbs.]; and a shield-bearer went before him. [8]Then he stood and cried out to the armies of Israel, and said to them, "Why have you come out to line up for battle? *Am I not a* Philistine, and you the servants of Saul [Israel's king]? Choose a man for yourselves, and let him come down to me. [9]If he is able to fight with me

and kill me, then we will be your servants. But if I prevail against him and kill him, then you shall be our servants and serve us." ¹⁰And the Philistine said, "I defy the armies of Israel this day; give me a man, that we may fight together." ¹¹When Saul and all Israel heard these words of the Philistine, they were dismayed and greatly afraid.

¹²Now David *was* the son of that Ephrathite of Bethlehem Judah, whose name *was* Jesse, and who had eight sons. And the man was old, advanced *in years,* in the days of Saul. ¹³The three oldest sons of Jesse had gone to follow Saul to the battle. The names of his three sons who went to the battle *were* Eliab the first-born, next to him Abinadab, and the third Shammah. ¹⁴David *was* the youngest. And the three oldest followed Saul. ¹⁵But David occasionally went and returned from Saul to feed his father's sheep at Bethlehem.

¹⁶And the Philistine drew near and presented himself forty days, morning and evening.

¹⁷Then Jesse said to his son David, "Take now for your brothers an ephah [3/5 of a bushel] of this dried *grain* and these ten loaves, and run to your brothers at the camp. ¹⁸And carry these ten cheeses to the captain of *their* thousand, and see how your brothers fare, and bring back news of them." ¹⁹Now Saul and they and all the men of Israel *were* in the Valley of Elah, fighting with the Philistines.

²⁰So David rose early in the morning, left the sheep with a keeper, and took *the things* and went as Jesse had commanded him. And he came to the camp as the army was going out to the fight and shouting for the battle. ²¹For Israel and the Philistines had drawn up in battle array, army against army. ²²And David left his supplies in the hand of the supply keeper, ran to the army, and came and greeted his brothers. ²³Then as he talked with them, there was the champion, the Philistine of Gath, Goliath by name, coming up from the armies of the Philistines; and he spoke according to the same words. So David heard *them.* ²⁴And all the men of Israel, when they saw the man, fled from him and were dreadfully afraid. ²⁵So the men of Israel said, "Have you seen this man who has come up? Surely he has come up to defy Israel; and it shall be *that* the man who kills him the king will enrich with great riches, will give him his daughter, and give his father's house exemption *from taxes* in Israel."

²⁶Then David spoke to the men who stood by him, saying, "What shall be done for the man who kills this Philistine and takes away the reproach from Israel? For who *is* this uncircumcised Philistine, that he should defy the armies of the living God?"

²⁷And the people answered him in this manner, saying, "So shall it be done for the man who kills him."

²⁸Now Eliab his oldest brother heard when he spoke to the men; and Eliab's anger was aroused against David, and he said, "Why did you come down here? And with whom have you left those few sheep in the wilderness? I know your pride and the insolence of your heart, for you have come down to see the battle."

²⁹And David said, "What have I done now? *Is there* not a cause?" ³⁰Then he turned from him toward another and said the same thing; and these people answered him as the first ones *did*.

³¹Now when the words which David spoke were heard, they reported *them* to Saul; and he sent for him. ³²Then David said to Saul, "Let no man's heart fail because of him; your servant will go and fight with this Philistine."

³³And Saul said to David, "You are not able to go against this Philistine to fight with him; for you *are* a youth, and he a man of war from his youth."

³⁴But David said to Saul, "Your servant used to keep his father's sheep, and when a lion or a bear came and took a lamb out of the flock, ³⁵I went out after it and struck it, and delivered *the lamb* from its mouth; and when it arose against me, I caught *it* by its beard, and struck and killed it. ³⁶Your servant has killed both lion and bear; and this uncircumcised Philistine will be like one of them, seeing he has defied the armies of the living God." ³⁷Moreover David said, "The LORD, who delivered me from the paw of the

lion and from the paw of the bear, He will deliver me from the hand of this Philistine."

And Saul said to David, "Go, and the LORD be with you!"

[38]So Saul clothed David with his armor, and he put a bronze helmet on his head; he also clothed him with a coat of mail. [39]David fastened his sword to his armor and tried to walk, for he had not tested *them*. And David said to Saul, "I cannot walk with these, for I have not tested *them*." So David took them off.

[40]Then he took his staff in his hand; and he chose for himself five smooth stones from the brook, and put them in a shepherd's bag, in a pouch which he had, and his sling was in his hand. And he drew near to the Philistine. [41]So the Philistine came, and began drawing near to David, and the man who bore the shield *went* before him. [42]And when the Philistine looked about and saw David, he disdained him; for he was *only* a youth, ruddy and good-looking. [43]So the Philistine said to David, "Am I a dog, that you come to me with sticks?" And the Philistine cursed David by his gods. [44]And the Philistine said to David, "Come to me, and I will give your flesh to the birds of the air and the beasts of the field!"

[45]Then David said to the Philistine, "You come to me with a sword, with a spear, and with a javelin. But I come to you in the name of the LORD of hosts, the God of the armies of Israel, whom you have defied. [46]This day the

LORD will deliver you into my hand, and I will strike you and take your head from you. And this day I will give the carcasses of the camp of the Philistines to the birds of the air and the wild beasts of the earth, that all the earth may know that there is a God in Israel. ⁴⁷Then all this assembly shall know that the LORD does not save with sword and spear; for the battle *is* the LORD's, and He will give you into our hands."

⁴⁸So it was, when the Philistine arose and came and drew near to meet David, that David hurried and ran toward the army to meet the Philistine. ⁴⁹Then David put his hand in his bag and took out a stone; and he slung *it* and struck the Philistine in his forehead, so that the stone sank into his forehead, and he fell on his face to the earth. ⁵⁰So David prevailed over the Philistine with a sling and a stone, and struck the Philistine and killed him. But *there was* no sword in the hand of David. ⁵¹Therefore David ran and stood over the Philistine, took his sword and drew it out of its sheath and killed him, and cut off his head with it.

And when the Philistines saw that their champion was dead, they fled. ⁵²Now the men of Israel and Judah arose and shouted, and pursued the Philistines as far as the entrance of the valley and to the gates of Ekron. And the wounded of the Philistines fell along the road to Shaaraim, even as far as Gath and Ekron. ⁵³Then the children of Israel returned from chasing the Philistines, and they plundered their tents. ⁵⁴And David took the head of the Philistine and brought it to Jerusalem, but he put his armor in his tent. (1 Samuel, 17:1-54)

David exhibited extreme courage because he had unshakeable faith that God would make him victorious and save the Israelites from the giant Philistines. Some people may say he was simply young and foolish. However, it cannot be said that David did not exhibit the highest level of courage. God had told the entire Israelite army He would give them victory over the Philistines, yet they stood, shaking in their sandals, afraid of the "giants" opposing them. They felt fighting the huge Philistines would be sure death. They didn't have the faith in God or the courage in their own abilities to face a larger foe.

So what if we aren't fighting the Philistines who God Himself had determined must die? What if our "Goliath" is a domineering boss, spouse, or coworkers who are difficult to get along with? What if we have an idea for a business but feel the responsibility of a family so strongly that we are afraid to step out and take a chance on being successful? Can we take courage in knowing that we can be as strong as anybody on the planet?

As a Christian, I espouse taking strength and courage from a relationship with Jesus, but I do understand that people also draw strength from other sources. We can draw faith from our confidence because of past success. We may have a very supportive spouse who believes in us and is a great encourager. Our parents may have filled us with a lifetime of courage because of their love and support in our endeavors. So ask yourself, from where do you get your strength? As with integrity, we all have courage. The question is how often do we exercise and strengthen courage? Before we dig deeper into the question of where can we take courage from, I'll offer a few more examples of extreme human courage.

Army lieutenant Audie Murphy grew up in hardscrabble Texas. His father had left the family when he was young, and his mother passed away when he was thirteen years old. The family was poor and usually hungry. He learned to shoot with a marksman's eye because he couldn't afford even two bullets some weeks, so his one bullet had to hit the mark. The squirrels he shot sustained the family for years.

On America's involvement in World War II, he lied about his age to enlist in any service that would take him. Being told he was too small for the marines and the navy, he enlisted in the army and became an infantryman. Lieutenant Murphy fought the enemy in countries all across Europe during WWII. He survived the war as one of the most, if not *the* most (there are varying accounts) highly decorated soldier, sailor, or marine during the war. He won the US Congressional Medal of Honor for one of his many extremely courageous acts of heroism.

In spite of his recognition for heroic acts, he remained extremely humble and very "matter of fact" about his exploits. His autobiography, *To Hell and Back*, details his experiences during the war. As stated previously, Lieutenant Murphy engaged in violent, close-up, in-your-face combat so often that he undoubtedly serves as one of the most credible American experts on the subjects of courage and fear and how a person can face them successfully.

His unit was preparing for yet another major assault against the Germans. His company was to clear a section of a highway where the Germans were entrenched on either side. He provides a breathtaking insight into how he dealt with the extremely valid fear of death and how he overcame it each time he was in battle.

> Stripped down to the essential equipment for combat, we advance by squads along the flanks of a dirt road that stretches toward enemy lines. The weather is sunny; and though it is January, beads of sweat roll from our skin. Fear is moving up with us.
>
> It always does. In the heat of battle it may go away. Sometimes it vanishes in a blind, red rage that comes when you see a friend fall. Then again you get so tired that you become indifferent. But when you are moving into combat, why try fooling yourself. Fear is right there beside you.
>
> Experience helps. You soon learn that a situation is seldom as black as the imagination paints it. Some always get through. Yes, but somebody gets it. You do not discuss the matter. It is quite personal. But the question keeps pounding through the brain:
>
> This time will I be the one that gets it?
>
> I am well acquainted with fear. It strikes first in the stomach, coming like a disemboweling hand that is thrust into the carcass of a chicken. I feel now as though icy fingers have reached into my mid-parts and twisted the intestines into knots.
>
> Each of us has his own way of fighting off panic. I recall Novak [his buddy who had been killed] and try working myself into a rage against the uniformed beings who killed him.

But that proves futile. At this distance the enemy is as impersonal as the gun that blew Little Mike's [Novak] pathetic dreams into eternity.

I turn my mind to faraway things: the meadows at home with the wind in the grass; a forgotten moment of laugher; a girl's face. But this also accomplishes nothing. The frosty fingers tighten their grip. Sweat drips from my forehead. (Murphy, 95–96)

Audie Murphy knew the reality of death and the fear that preceded battle. However, Lieutenant Audie Murphy thought about the fear, strove to understand it, and even learned to embrace the fear. Fear was a familiar acquaintance to Lieutenant Murphy, yet he had the courage to rise above his fear and face death in a noble and valiant manner.

Although I wrote about Senator John McCain earlier, I want to introduce you to another man who belongs to a group of people I consider the biggest heroes and mentally strongest people in existence. I believe any former American POW is courage personified. We've all heard of Lieutenant Louis Zamperini, an American World War II airplane bombardier who survived forty-five days adrift on a raft in the Pacific after his plane went down, only to be "rescued" by the Japanese. He became a POW for the next two years. Louie Zamperini and the other WWII POWs survived starvation, freezing cold temperatures, beatings, and mental and physical torture. Lieutenant Zamperini's story became well known from Laura Hildenbrand's book *Unbroken*, and the later movie by the same title. In Vietnam, men like Senator John McCain, Admiral Jeremiah Denton, General Robinson Risner, Admiral James Stockdale, Colonel George "Bud" Day, Captain Everette

Alvarez (over nine years in captivity), and more than 350 other American heroes exhibited great courage in merely surviving each day also. The book *When Hell Was in Session*, by Jeremiah Denton, is mind-numbing and awe-inspiring in its accounts of what then Commander Denton survived as a Vietnam POW. Jeremiah Denton later retired from the navy as a rear admiral (one-star) and then served as a US senator representing Alabama.

Commander Denton was shot down during a combat mission near Thanh Hoah, North Vietnam, on July 18, 1965. He was one of the first dozen pilots shot down and taken prisoner. They were primarily held in the Hoa Lo Prison in Hanoi, North Vietnam, but there were other prisons the POWs were sometimes rotated to. Of course, the American POWs quickly renamed the Hoa Lo prison in their euphemistic, albeit sarcastic [well-earned sarcasm, by the way] vernacular as the Hanoi Hilton (Denton, 21).

Commander Denton, and his American prison-mates, who were mainly air force and navy pilots who had been shot down over North Vietnam during combat missions and bombing raids, soon began arguably the most demanding, brutal, painful, barbaric, gut-wrenching, and tortuous existences in captivity that have ever been documented. In my mind, American POWs from WWII and Vietnam and concentration camp survivors from Nazi Germany in WWII are absolutely in the top tier of the mentally strongest people that have ever existed. In 1992 I bought a silver POW/Missing in Action (MIA) bracelet while stationed in San Antonio. I've worn it ever since as a sign of respect and remembrance to all American POWs and all airmen, sailors, soldiers, and marines who have fought the enemy on behalf of the United States.

In 1955 President Dwight Eisenhower had the Code of

Conduct created as a way to give American POWs guidance when/if they become prisoners of war. The code is a brilliant reference for POWs to memorize and then try to live out to the best of their ability during captivity. Explicitly stated in the code are the instructions that POWs should resist the enemy by all means available. That resistance applies to oral and written statements, and any other efforts by the enemy to obtain propaganda that would be favorable to their cause and harmful to America and its allies.

Commander Denton and several other POWs, including those I mentioned earlier, soon become known as strong resisters and strong in encouraging the other POWs to resist. Naturally, they became favorite targets of the North Vietnamese for torture and other deprivations, although nobody but the few outright traitors who sought their own comfort above all else avoided torture, squalid living conditions, and deprivation.

The torture the POWs endured defies human comprehension, yet they continued to fight their captors, showing unheard of courage each time they resisted giving information as long as humanly possible. One of many instances of Commander Denton's courage and resistance is symbolic of the hundreds of times he and other POWs resisted giving their captures vital military information or even nonconsequential biographical information. To freely provide *any* information other than the name, rank, service number, and date of birth was considered to be cooperating with the enemy and contrary to the Code of Conduct.

In April of 1966, Commander Denton and all POWs were continually asked "to write" by their North Vietnamese captors. What they were asked to write could be anything from a confession to being a war criminal and bombing North

Vietnam, giving military information, giving the names of other pilots in the units they were with when they were shot down, or even biographical information about their childhood, friends, and family. The North Vietnamese were extremely skilled at turning any information provided into propaganda to trick the world into thinking the POWs were being treated kindly. Or they would use the information as leverage to pry more information or propaganda material out of the POWs at a later date. Commander Denton was being starved and held in solitary confinement when he was asked to write the names of his squadron mates; he refused.

The following story exemplifies the sheer courage Commander Denton displayed in the face of unspeakable torture.

> On April 20 I again refused to write. Dog [one of the guards] accused me of "inciting others to resist" and said that I would be sent back to Hoa Lo [the Hilton], where I would be tortured until I confessed my crimes.
>
> In half an hour, I was on my way back to the Hanoi Hilton. I had barely enough time to pass the word about my destination and the reason for my move. Although I wasn't thirsty, I drank all the water in my jug. I didn't expect to get food or water for a long time. I also learned just before I left the grim news that [Robinson] Risner had been tortured for a confession at the Hilton.
>
> Upon arriving at the Hilton, I was turned over to a guard that I hadn't seen before. His nickname, I learned later, was Pigeye. He was a cold, bloodless professional, a master torturer

who knew all the ways to apply painful techniques. He was considered an expert, and all the prisoners came to fear him.

Pigeye was a senior enlisted man in his early thirties. He spoke and wrote Chinese and spoke some English. He had probably been educated in China. His angular face was marked by high cheekbones, but its dominant feature was a thin, hard mouth that could only be described as cruel in the most classic sense.

He immediately took me to the Knobby Room, a 20-by-20-foot cell that got its name from the knobs of concrete on the walls which helped to soundproof it. There was a desk on one side of the room and two ordinary, four-legged stools on the other side. I watched as he placed one stool on top of the other. He assisted me to a sitting position on the top stool, cuffed my hands tightly behind me, and left the room. I was in a precarious position, 5 feet above the cement floor, with no way to break my fall if I should topple off.

Pigeye had been brisk and emotionless in his actions, I knew the North Vietnamese were not fooling around. They intended to break me for a confession. I settled down for a long wait, blinking up occasionally at the single bare light bulb that Pigeye had left burning, but mostly just sitting there staring straight ahead. I was prepared to wait them out.

It soon became apparent they were trying to starve a confession from me. For three days and nights I went without food or water. I sat on the stools, shifting my position carefully from time to time to ease the strain on my back and shoulder muscles, praying hard.

As some point, I simply had to urinate, and I carefully toppled the stools so that I could land on my feet. I opened the peephole in the door with my nose, stood on top of the stool, and urinated through the hole. Fortunately, there was no guard around, but unfortunately, I couldn't arrange the stools so I could get back on them. I deliberately scraped my cheek on the wall and then lay down on the floor in a heap, pretending that I'd fallen asleep and dropped off the stools. When Pigeye came to check on me, he let my presence on the floor pass, although he must have been suspicious of the puddle outside the door. He sat me back on the stools.

I began hallucinating during the second night. At times the knobs on the walls became faces, sometimes devils, sometimes angels. The devils would come screaming and taunting; the angels would be singing and playing their harps. My only firm and constant thought was that I would die of starvation before I would write a confession.

On the third evening, Rabbit came into the room. Rabbit was a young officer, his most memorable feature being rather prominent front teeth. He was intelligent and spoke good English. He was proud of being a party [Communist] member, and if one appealed to his ego, he could sometimes be drawn into revealing more than he should. He used the standard alternating good-guy, bad-guy technique. That evening he was being the good-guy. He said he thought that torture was the wrong way and had tried to alter the approach.

"But I tell you man to man, Denton," he said. "They are going to torture you tomorrow if you do not write a confession. I know you will not give into starvation. I have told them that. They will hurt you very badly. Maybe they will kill you," he said.

I said that I would not write anything.

Rabbit argued at length with me. "Denton, my government will probably not even use the confession. Maybe no one will ever read it. My government knows that it is humiliating for you to write a confession even if the confession is forced, and not credible. They hope the suffering will cause you to act more reasonable, but they will probably not publicize your confession. You have everything to gain and nothing to lose if you write it. Your treatment will greatly improve; you will even get a roommate. Aren't you lonely after ten months alone?" [Commander Denton and several other POWs would eventually live in solitary confinement for over four years in total.]

I told him again that I would not write.

He sighed and shrugged his shoulders. "We will allow you to rest some time tonight. You have until morning to change your mind," he said, and left.

I concluded that he was trying to provide me with a face-saving way to give in early during the torture the next day, by consoling myself that I had done enough in withstanding the starvation treatment. He succeeded only in increasing my resolve.

That night I was taken to Cell 1 in New Guy Village, where Pigeye placed my arms in two stocks suspended between bunks in such a position that I could neither stand nor kneel. After several hours, Rabbit came back with a guard, who took me out of the stocks and told me to lie down on one of the bunks and sleep. I was also given four crackers and some tea, but they failed to whet my appetite, as the Vietnamese had apparently hoped.

At some point, I discovered that Jim Stockdale was a couple of cells away and called out to him. I had nothing to lose. I talked openly to Stockdale and told him what had been going on at the Zoo. I gave him a message for Jane [Commander Denton's wife] in case he got home. I wanted her to get married again. My love for her was so great that I could even love the man she married.

I explained to Stockdale that Catholics believed that martyrs go straight to Heaven and I hoped God would consider my death a martyrdom because I would be killed by an atheistic government which was trying to force me to renounce my God-fearing government. I was convinced that the next day would be my last on earth, and I felt no bitterness. God had given me a full life.

The next morning, the ominous figure of Pigeye appeared in my cell door. He was accompanied by two guards. He asked me if I had changed my mind. I told him no. Without further conversation, I was pulled from my cell and taken to Room 18, also known as the Meathook Room. Pigeye and one of the other guards grasped me, handcuffed my hands behind me, and then, grunting and swearing, began beating me severely. I tried to keep my feet and appear impassive as their fists thumped into my body and face, but it was impossible. I reeled about the cell and fell down repeatedly. They kept pulling me to my feet and hitting me, but this type of punishment always angered more than intimidated me. Bloody nose, cut lips, blackened eyes, bruised ribs: the standard preliminary before the main event.

Then there was a welcome pause. Sitting on the floor, I shook my head and focused my eyes. There was a thin rope in Pigeye's hands, and I felt something like relief. I was ready to lose my arms rather than shed my honor, and I wanted to get it over with. He pulled my shirt sleeves down to protect my arms from scars (at that point, they were still hoping to keep the torture secret so they could say our writings were voluntary), and then he and another guard began roping one arm from shoulder to elbow. With each loop, one guard would put his foot on my arm and pull, another guard joining him in the effort to draw the rope as tightly as their combined strengths would permit. The other arm was then bound, and both were tied together so closely that the elbows touched.

The first pains were from the terrible pinching of the flesh. After about ten minutes, an agonizing pain began to flow through the arms and shoulders as my heart struggled to pump blood through the strangled veins. After about forty-five minutes, the pain began to subside and I began to go numb. I was too weak to sit up, and when I fell backward, the weight of my body spread my fingers so grotesquely that two of them were dislocated.

Pigeye had begun to lose his celebrated composure by now. His face was animated and covered with sweat, and he was apparently afraid I would outlast them and beat them out of their confession. They had cuffed a cement filled 9-foot-long iron bar across my ankles, and Pigeye released the bar from the shackles and laid it across my shins. He stood on it, and he and the other guard took turns jumping up and down and rolling it across my legs. Then they lifted my arms behind my back by the cuffs, raising the top part of my body off the floor and dragging me around and around. This went on for hours.

They were in a frenzy, alternating the treatment to increase the pain until I was unable to control myself. I began crying hysterically, blood and tears mingling and running down my cheeks. I feigned unconsciousness several times, but Pigeye was too much of an expert for that. He merely lifted the lids over my eyes and grinned.

Finally, I had nothing left. My only thought was a desire to be free of pain. I tried to shout but I could only whisper, "Bao cao, bao cao," the words for surrender. The last thing I remembered before passing out was the smile on Pigeye's face as he continued to roll the bar across my legs.

When I awakened, I was sitting naked on the floor in an unfamiliar shower room, a guard propping me up while Pigeye watched. Cold water mixed with blood as it ran down the drain. Pigeye said, "Wash," and he and the other guard left me sitting there rolling on the floor in the water and blood. As I slapped limply at my swollen wrists, trying to restore the circulation. I heard a voice say, "Hey, ol' buddy, what's your name?"

My voice was practically gone, and I couldn't be heard over the sound of the shower. I struggled to my knees and managed to turn it off with my elbow. I said as loud as I could, "I'm Denton."

"Jeremiah Denton?"

I said yes.

"God bless you, Jeremiah Denton. You did a wonderful job at the Zoo." He identified himself as Robbie Risner and told me I was in the shower at Heartbreak Hotel. He was in a cell across the hall.

I said something to the effect that I wasn't doing a very good job now.

"You are only human," he said. (Denton, 62–66)

Sometime after this brutal period of interrogation, Commander Denton was again pushed to the end of his endurance. After going through what he had already been through, you would think he would have quickly obliged and given the Vietnamese whatever information they wanted. But Commander Denton, and most all of the Vietnam POWs like him, stiffened their resolute defiance and called upon what are some of the most incredible examples of mental and physical strength and unmatched courage, and resisted the enemy time and time again. They resisted giving any information, knowing they would be tortured in the most heinous ways imaginable, even to the point of death. They simply knew it was against the Code of Conduct, and the information could be used to hurt their POW brethren. Any information given could also be dangerous to their brethren who were still flying and fighting the enemy.

I cannot imagine waking up in the morning as Commander Denton did on that day of the interrogation, and thinking that I was going to be tortured until I died that day. Yet that's what Commander Denton felt, and he still maintained his resolve to not give the enemy any useful information, even if it meant he would die.

Over the course of history, millions of people have gone to their deaths for their countries while exhibiting unmatched courage. Hundreds of thousands of Christians have been martyred for their faith in Jesus Christ, yet they have stood firm in their faith, knowing they would likely soon die for their faith. Tens of millions of people have gone to their figurative deaths over time facing their boss over a question of integrity or standing up to an abusive spouse. Each human being has within them the ability to live out the courage of a thousand warriors. We *all* have that courage, as I previously said. We just need to set our minds to do it… to act with the courage that we so badly want to act with. I understand it's one of those things that is easier said than done. We need to tell that fear within us to get behind us, and press on in doing what we know we need to do, with courage.

Later in his book, while recounting yet another horrific torture session, Commander Denton gives this beautiful account of how he obtained peace, strength, and further courage to endure yet another marathon torture session.

> By the fifth morning, I was nearing despair. I offered myself to God with an admission that I could take no more on my own. Tears ran down my face as I repeated my vow of surrender to Him. Strangely, as soon as I made the vow, a deep feeling of peace settled into my tortured mind and pain-wracked body, and the suffering left me completely. It was the most profound and deeply inspiring moment of my life. (Denton, 93)

I will not minimize the struggles that each of us face in our daily lives. Sometimes, even if just in our minds, our struggles are equal to or exceed those of US POWs or WWII concentration camp prisoners. I offer that if we can just try to look at the situation objectively and consider the countless situations that others have courageously triumphed over, perhaps that situation will lesson in importance. I pray we can strive to find a positive aspect of the situation, thank God for the good things He has given us, and pray for courage to withstand the bad.

Please remember, though, we can never judge what causes another person to perform at work the way they do, either good or bad. I like to recite the common phrase of, "We can never judge a person until we've walked a mile in their shoes." We simply don't know what hardships they may be experiencing in their home lives. Sadly, significant troubles with spouses and children are more common than we think. Obviously, the issues at home will likely affect the person's work performance. We as leaders definitely need to address the performance. However, we need to remember there is a real human being with real-life issues on the other end of the conversation. We need to treat that person with respect and compassion even if their performance requires discipline.

General George S. Patton Jr. is also a remarkable, albeit different, example of leadership and exhibiting courage over fear regardless of the cost. General Patton's executive officer in the early years of World War II was Lieutenant Porter B. Williamson. Lieutenant Williamson was selected for pilot training and did not accompany General Patton overseas to the actual fighting, but served under him as General Patton prepared soldiers to fight at the Desert Training Center in the Mojave Desert in California. Lieutenant Williamson very much appreciated General Patton's leadership, teaching abilities, and overall mentorship. He captured the leadership traits and successful living principles in the book *Patton's Principles*. In his book, Lieutenant Williamson states that he feels he captured the real leadership essence and General Patton's care for his fellow man better than most of the hundreds of biographies of General Patton that are in existence. General Patton also appreciated Mr. Williamson's personality, hard work ethic, and ability to get things done. In fact, General Patton's son, Major General George S. Patton III, stated to Mr. Williamson, "I know my dad would be proud to have his principles sorted out by you" (Williamson, 6).

Before General Colin Powell said it, General George S. Patton said, "Never take counsel of your fears." Mr. Williamson quotes General Patton as saying, "There is a time to take counsel of your fears, and there is a time never to listen to any fear. It is always important to know what you are doing." General Patton admonished,

> The time to take counsel of your fears is before you make an important battle decision. That's the time to listen to every fear you can imagine! When you have collected all of the facts and fears and made your decision, turn-off all of your fears and go ahead!" He continued, "Every plan you make in war is going to be a live-or-die decision. You will either live or die as a result of your decision. Since we are not afraid to do either there is no reason to take counsel of our fears."
>
> He continued, "The chance of being killed in combat is not as great as being killed on our highways. If you want to take counsel of your fears, stop driving that car! And don't crawl in bed at night! More people die in bed than any other place!" We laughed.

When there was time, Gen. Patton explained his ideas, saying, "The person who cannot face death has truly never faced life because every day of life is a day closer to death. To take counsel of fears about death is to destroy every day of living." (Williamson, 81)

In fact, General Patton talked of fear and death quite often. He said, "Fear makes us stronger. Every time we whip a fear we will get a bigger fear. We can take any fear if we are not fearful of death. One thing is for sure we will all live until we die. Some of us die from fear but our breathing could go on for years. There is more to life than breathing. Death has to be the best part of living" (Williamson, 159)!

General Patton's philosophy was that those who live in fear will die a thousand deaths. He said, "A coward is always in eternal torment because he will suffer a thousand deaths every day. A brave man will only die once! When you have the faith to fight something to death, there is no death. Death will be only a phase in the cycle of life" (Williamson, 157).

Another legendary American POW during the Vietnam conflict was air force colonel George "Bud" Day, who I've mentioned already. Colonel Day grew up in eastern Iowa (Go Hawkeyes!) and had enlisted in the marines during WWII. He needed a waiver to enlist due to being smaller and younger than the minimum entrance standards, but his desire to serve and do what he felt was his duty to the United States pushed him through many obstacles. He grew up in the poor side of town where very few young people went to college or ever became successful in any endeavor. After being discharged from the marines, he later joined the Army National Guard and then the Air Force Reserves before coming onto air force active duty in March of 1951 (Coram, 61).

Colonel Day's life history is one of the most amazing stories there is in American history of courage, persistence, and the pursuit of perfection. I referenced the book *American Patriot, the Life and Wars of Colonel Bud Day* when I wrote about Senator John McCain. This book is also one of the all-time best books I've ever read about leadership. Even though he developed a reputation for being calm under pressure, Colonel Day also had a hot temper that gained him notoriety in many instances throughout his life. Regardless, in everything he did prior to service, during his service, and post-service, he exemplified a dedication to his family, the military, fellow POWs, and brothers-in-arms. As a pilot, he was known to be very proficient and strict about adherence to the rules. As a POW, he was known to be among the fiercest resisters and staunchest supporter and leader of his fellow POWs. In fact, he earned the US Medal of Honor for his leadership and re- sistance as a POW. While the stories of the torture sessions he endured are equally, if not more, graphic and legendary than those of Admiral Denton, I'll focus the next few paragraphs on his courage when it came to defending his men against poor leadership above him. His defense of his men could have meant losing his most treasured and sought after job in the air force, that of a combat squadron commander. However, his courage to withstand interrogation as a POW is bone-chilling and awesomely inspiring, so I provide a story of his strength and courage in interrogation a little bit later.

In March of 1966, Colonel Day arrived in Vietnam as a forward air controller (FAC). These men flew deep into enemy territory, facing all manner of missile, rocket, and small-arms fire to find and report valuable enemy targets. Because of his leadership and flying acumen, Colonel Day was given command of a new FAC unit that would fly very fast (FACs usually flew slower planes to give them more time to see potential targets) aircraft and routinely fly through the most heavily defended airspace in North Vietnam (Coram, 121).

Even though Colonel Day had misgivings about flying the particular aircraft they flew in a FAC capacity, he poured his heart and soul into the mission and his men. Colonel Day named the unit after his favorite song, "Misty."

> For about a week after Misty cranked up, it was just as Day had feared: targets were impossible to find. But after maybe a half dozen flights, the Mistys not only knew the AO (Area of Operations) intimately but began to see the hand of man against the natural jungle. They saw tracks on the road still glistening with water and knew a vehicle had recently passed. They saw faint condensation from a truck exhaust at dawn, anomalies in camouflage that revealed it was not real, or could pick out the shape of a gun battery under the camouflage. They developed "Misty eyes": they could see what other pilots could not see.
>
> "Hit my smoke" [the confident way Mistys had of accurately calling out targets] and high-value targets became the hallmarks of the Mistys; that and their aggressive nature. Indeed, everything about the Mistys was a reflection of Day's leadership. Tigers breed tigers.

> "Misty" would become a call-sign of mythic proportions, one of the most famous of the Vietnam War. (Coram, 125)

As the commander of a new unit, Colonel Day developed and wrote air force doctrine for jet FACs. As usual, he was more concerned about the safety, welfare, and success of his men than about his own advancement.

> One morning Day took off before dawn and found the AO covered with patch fog and a low cloud deck – a recipe for disaster. A gunner needs to know the course, altitude and speed of his target. The course of the aircraft was obvious. A gunner could look through the patch fog and estimate with considerable accuracy the altitude of the cloud bottoms. Had a Misty come in skimming the bottoms of the clouds, the gunner would know his altitude within a hundred feet or so. AAA [Anti-Aircraft Artillery] gunners in North Vietnam were some of the most experienced in the world. Thus, low clouds and fog sandwiched an aircraft into a narrow zone from which it would be almost impossible to escape.
>
> Plus, a Misty would not see AAA or missiles until they popped through the fog, and by then it was too late to maneuver.
>
> Day returned to Phu Cat and postponed the outgoing flight until the fog lifted.
>
> A few minutes later, the vice wing commander, a full colonel, banged open the door

of the Misty office, accosted Day, and said, "I have frag orders for Route Pack One" [frag orders are fragmentary orders, a brief outline of the mission].

"I just came from up there," Day said. "The weather is too low."

The colonel raised his voice. "You don't get it, Major. That's a Seventh Air Force TOT [time on target] and you have to meet it. Get that aircraft in the air."

Bill Douglass and several other Mistys were in the room and moved away, but they listened.

Day moved so close to the colonel that their noses were about four inches apart. "YOU don't get it, Colonel. I don't care what Seventh Air Force says. My men are not going."

The colonel stomped out. Douglass and the young pilots looked at one another. They had a boss who would risk his career for his men. The incident became part of the legend of Misty 1 [Colonel Day's call sign]. (Coram, 129–130)

Lastly, after being shot down on a Misty FAC mission, as stated previously, Colonel Day resisted so strongly and resolutely that he won the Medal of Honor for his leadership and resistance as a POW. Even before Colonel Day became a resident of the Hanoi Hilton, he became famous for escaping his initial captors while they were moving him across the country to the Hilton. Though he had been severely injured in his ejection, he willed himself to escape and evade for twelve to fifteen days. He was starved, deliriously in pain, and dehydrated to the point of near death, yet he still walked countless miles south toward South

Vietnam and freedom. After many days on the lam and only an hour or so from freedom, he was recaptured. True to his integrity, character, and toughness, and instead of quitting and giving up, he strengthened his resolve for the unknown horrors he would face for almost six years.

> The POWs recall the summer of 1969 as the time of the most vicious, systematic, and sustained torture of their long imprisonment. A new camp commander mandated the guards to seal the light and airholes in each cell. The temperature was well over 100 degrees, and POWs sweltered in a darkness that only increased their apprehension. Day and night the shrill and sustained screams of American pilots echoed through the prisons of North Vietnam. The very jangling of a guard's keys made strong men tremble. They prayed the guard was coming for someone else, and then they were racked with both guilt if another man was taken to torture and dread because next time the guard would come for them.
>
> The harshest reprisals were visited upon senior officers who the guards thought were the brains behind the escape attempt [two POWs attempted to escape in early 1969, they were quickly captured] but who in reality, for security reasons, had not been told in advance. Until the summer of 1969, putting a prisoner in the ropes was considered the most painful and debilitating of all forms of torture. But this time the torture was different. A four-foot-long

rubber strip cut from a tire was used to beat the Americans. They called it the "fan belt."

Day felt a special apprehension. He was the Senior Ranking Officer of a building called the Barn and he realized he soon would be facing the greatest trial of his life. Midwesterners know two things for certain. The first is how to reduce complex issues down to the basics. So, in the quiet before the guards came for him, Day made a solemn vow, a simple vow of three parts:

I will not do or say or write anything that will embarrass Doris [Colonel Day's wife] and the children.

I will not do or say or write anything that will embarrass the Air Force.

I will not do or say or write anything that will embarrass my country.

Day knew that, God willing, someday this would all be over, and if he was still alive, he would go home. On that day, he was determined to hold his head high.

Return with Honor.

That would be his creed.

He would die before he dishonored his family, the Air Force, or his country.

If he could not return with honor, he would not return at all.

The second thing Midwesterners know about is fortitude. In his *Maxim of War*, Napoleon says, "The first qualification of a soldier is fortitude under fatigue and privation." Most people think courage should be the first qualification, but without fortitude to survive the terrible times that sometimes are the lot of the soldier, he may not be able to reach the place where courage is required. From his father, Bud Day learned all there was to know about fortitude.

Early on Wednesday morning, July 16, Day heard the jangle of the guard's keys. The door opened and it was his time.

Like every POW, he thought this might be a mistake, that there would be some sort of intervention, or that his captors would change their minds. But as the guard marched him out of the room, Day looked over his shoulder and saw a second guard pick up the small towel that every POW had in his cell.

Being marched off in the predawn darkness toward torture does things to a man's mind. Cold fear knotted Day's stomach and his knees trembled.

Inside the small blood-spattered quiz [interrogation] room, a guard stood against one wall holding a fan belt. On the opposite wall another guard also held a fan belt.

A guard motioned and said, "Drop pants."

Extremely tight and painful hand cuffs were ratcheted deep into his wrists. Almost immediately his hands began to swell. Irons were clamped around his ankles.

July temperatures in Hanoi, even at dawn, are around 80 degrees. Nevertheless, as Day's pajamas fell to his ankles, he shivered. He was naked before his enemies. And he knew enough about pain to know that eventually he could be made to talk. "If you torture me, I will lie," he told the guards. "And later, I will take it all back. I will withdraw whatever I say."

One guard ripped the small towel in half and forced it into Day's mouth.

"Down!" a guard shouted.

Day slumped to his knees and then to his stomach and realized no questions had been asked. This was not about information. This was about torture.

Dear God, give me strength. Give me strength. Let me endure. Please, God. Don't let me talk. Please.

A guard across the room stood erect, tightened his grip on the fan belt, and grunted as he pushed off from the wall. He raised the belt high above his head and used the momentum of his dash across the room to smash the belt across Day's buttocks.

The towel did not muffle the noise. Day's scream sliced through the dawn, the POWs knew another American had been called to torture.

While that scream still hung in the air, the second guard launched from the wall and brought his fan belt down on Day's buttocks.

One scream merged into another as the guards bounced from wall to wall. From some distant remote place, Day realized the sound of the fan belt on his skin was crisp and sharp.

Hour after hour the beating continued, the lashes falling from Day's buttocks to his thighs and then up over his lower back, and after a while the sound of the belt hitting his flesh changed into a soft splatting sound and then to a wet plopping noise.

God, give me strength. Don't let me talk. Please, God.

Occasionally, when the guards needed a break, the interrogator asked, "Are you ready to confess your black crimes?"

Each time Day shook his head no, and the beating continued.

He was frequently reminded that he was a Yankee air pirate with a bad attitude.

Sometime in late morning the beating stopped so Day could eat, so he could have strength to endure the afternoon session. He slowly sipped the thin pumpkin soup and cup of water.

The men who had beaten Day were tired, and two new guards came in and gripped the fan belts and the session resumed. Late in the afternoon, when these guards were too tired to continue, Day was dragged to his cell and given another bowl of pumpkin soup.

All he wanted was rest and sleep and to renew his strength for what would come with the new day. But he had not finished his soup when he was ordered to his knees, and the leg irons and painful hand cuffs were reapplied. When the guards finished screwing down the cuffs into Day's swollen wrists, blood was flowing freely. He was kept on his knees all night. Every time his head nodded in exhaustion, he was prodded with a bayonet.

On the morning of the second day, the torture resumed. Sometime that morning the three hundredth lash from the fan belt fell on Day's buttocks. He lost count after that, too groggy from lack of sleep and too weak to keep track. Guards asked him about the hierarchy of the Pentagon and the CIA, two subjects that obsessed the North Vietnamese and two topics that invariably came up during a torture session. Day had never served in the Pentagon and knew little about the CIA.

The beatings continued.

Dear God, give me strength.

He spent that night on his knees. Because he was so tired and weak, the bayonet pokes were more frequent.

By the third day the shackles had cut so deeply into his ankles that his Achilles tendons were visible. The shiny white of his patella could be seen on both knees.

On the morning of the fourth day, after Day spent another sleepless night on his knees, the guard shouted, "Are you ready to confess your black crimes?"

"I hope your mother dies [a very shameful death]," Day replied.

The beating continued.

Now the guards stood at Day's feet when they beat him. The fan belts sliced into his private areas.

Please. Strength.

That evening he was tottering back and forth on his knees and being prodded so often with the bayonet that the guard ordered him to sit on a stool. Within seconds he fell asleep and slumped to the floor. During the subsequent beating, the guard broke two of Day's front teeth, cutting his own knuckles in the process. This made the guard quite angry, and he slapped Day so hard that he ruptured the prisoner's eardrum.

When Day was dragged off to the quiz room on the morning of the sixth day, his buttocks and thighs were swollen and puffed out about three inches. Atop the hamburger-like flesh, from the middle of his thighs up to the small of his back, a scab was trying to form. Day's lower legs were twice their normal size, and his toes were overstuffed sausages. A watery fluid oozed from his private areas.

The leg irons and painful hand cuffs were forced on him.

He dropped his pants and slumped to the floor on the wet place where his blood was trying to congeal atop that of other POWs.

He was forced deep into himself, to the very core of his being. In that dark hour he found the rock to which he would cling, the words that symbolized his deepest beliefs and his deepest desire. If he died, these words would be his last thought.

Return with Honor.

That day he did what every POW did under sustained torture. He broke. He knew he had been crippled for life. He knew he was at the point of death. So he talked. But when he talked, he offered only lies. When the interrogator wanted to know about various escape committees and their functions, Day said there was a transportation committee whose job it was to line up trucks to haul POWs out of Hanoi after the next escape. He gave them the names of every committee that every military organization for two hundred years had formed, information so trivial and so frivolous that he was amazed the guards accepted it.

"Who are the committee members?"

"I am the only member of each committee."

The fan belts ripped the scab from his back and flayed his private areas. He said everyone in his building was on every committee, an equal impossibility.

Return with Honor.

That night he was ordered back on the stool. His buttocks were so raw he could not sit on them, so he sat at an angle on his hips. When he fell asleep he was beaten and put on his knees.

Sometime during that long night, he began excruciating, painful and uncontrollable vomiting. He slumped in a pool of blood and vomit and body waste.

The guards were disgusted.

Return with Honor.

The guard put him on his knees. When he collapsed, the guard beat him until he awakened.

It was not his battered body that he thought about that night. He knew that if he lived, one day the pain would end. But the suffering that came with violating the Code of Conduct would last forever. Never mind that everything he told his guards was fiction or useless information. Never mind that every POW sooner or later talked to the enemy. All Bud Day could think of was that he had gone beyond name, rank, serial number, and date of birth: the Big Four. He was ashamed of himself, and his suffering knew no limits.

The next morning the guard looked at the stinking scarecrow before him and asked, "How do you think of your treatment by the humane and lenient Vietnamese people?"

"My treatment is brutal, uncivilized, inhumane, and far below the standards of the Geneva Convention."

"Drop pants."

The guards knew Day was at the point of death, and the beatings lessened in severity. Still, July became August and the beatings continued. The guards wanted Day to write a statement saying the war was immoral. But Day did not have the luxury of free speech that civilians had; he was a serving military officer in the hands of the enemy, and he was bound by the Code of Conduct. He did what he did with full knowledge of the consequences.

"I can't do that."

As the beating began, he shut his eyes, his mind traveled to a different place, and he held on to his rock:

Return with Honor.

By now the guard and Day had fallen into a verbal shorthand.

"Write or not?"

"No write. Never."

"You write."

"No."

"Drop pants."

The beatings continued on a daily basis, but now he received maybe a dozen lashes. Years later he would remember and say, "Happiness is a short quiz."

Sometime near mid-September the beatings ended and Day was dragged off to solitary. The door was barely closed before he crawled to the wall and began tapping that he had been in daily quiz for months and was in bad shape physically and mentally. "Do not send any camp news," he said. "I don't want to know anything that might get someone else tortured."

Larry Guarino tapped back that Day had made his country proud, that he had performed as a U.S. military officer should perform by continuing to be strong. He ended by saying that twenty-six POWs had been beaten to the edge of death. But a few days later, Air Force major Leo Thorsness [author of an inspiring book entitled *Surviving Hell: A POW's Journey*] tapped a message saying that none of the men in the Barn had been tortured because of anything that Day said during the quiz.

Day wept. (Coram, 208–215)

When I read the stories of courage, toughness, integrity, and honor that US POWs—and, of course, all service members who have been in combat—have endured over the course of American history, I am as awestruck as a little boy is when he gets to chance to meet a legendary sports figure. Remember the Coke commercial from the 1980s when the little boy meets "Mean" Joe Greene from the Pittsburgh Steelers in the stadium tunnel and gives him his bottle of Coke? Joe downs the Coke in one long swig. Remember the pure awe in the little boy's eyes when Mean Joe thanks the little boy by giving him his game-day jersey? That's how I feel when I read about courageous American service members.

I love what God says in Deuteronomy 31:6: "Be strong and of good courage, do not fear nor be afraid of them; for the Lord your God, He is the One who goes with you. He will not leave you nor forsake you." I also love what God says in Matthew 10:28: "And do not fear those who kill the body but cannot kill the soul. But rather fear Him who is able to destroy both soul and body in hell."

As I've matured, I've sought to more and more build my faith in God and have no fear of what mere humans can do to me. That doesn't mean I never have fears, but when life's difficulties are placed into the bigger picture of God's love and His offer of a life in Heaven with Him through a relationship with Jesus Christ, it's easier to worry a little less and look to the future with more hope and anticipation.

CHAPTER 5

HUMBLENESS

sn't it funny how we can exhibit humbleness ourselves, or sometimes it can be forced upon us? During the time I slugged, I did find it to be a somewhat humbling experience. Here I was, a professional airman in the world's greatest air force, and I was bumming for a ride! When looking across the average slug line, I saw a mixture of middle-class to upper-middle-class society. It's safe to say, given the proximity to Washington DC, that a majority of slugs were probably college educated and worked in government jobs. Although certainly some slugs worked in purely civilian occupations, many were active duty military, government service civilians, or contractors with defense contractor companies. The bottom line is that these people, many of them with bachelor's, master's, or even doctoral degrees, were all in the same line waiting to bum a ride from a complete stranger!

In fact, many people wore their military uniforms and were fairly high ranking. I saw the highest enlisted paygrades (E9) and multiple fairly high-ranking lieutenant colonels (O5) or even colonels (O6) waiting in line. Of course, I also saw high-ranking navy officers in line, be they commanders (O5) or captains (O6). These military professionals, by nature of their rank, all led or supervised anywhere from tens to hundreds to thousands of people. Despite their positions, they allowed themselves to be humbled by being slugs, waiting to essentially hitchhike with someone.

As stated earlier, regardless of how important someone was at work, regardless of how many millions of dollars they controlled, and regardless of how many people worked for them, they all were willing to ride in the backseat of a Honda Civic or Ford Escort! They were willing to be cramped and perhaps even get their nice work clothes or uniforms covered in dog or cat hair because the driver either forgot to clean the seat or just plain didn't bother to!

When I think of humble leaders in history, of course a certain Jewish carpenter by the name of Jesus Christ lives the forefront of my mind. Not only did the Savior of the universe humbly begin life on earth as fully God and fully a man yet completely dependent little baby, He continued His role as a humble servant-leader His entire short life (thirty-three years) on earth. He chose the uneducated in society (fishermen for the most part) to be His disciples. He allowed Himself to be baptized by John the Baptist when He was in actuality the Son of God. Another extremely humble example Jesus set for His disciples was to wash their feet to teach them to serve each other and humanity in general (John 13:1–17). Please remember, in the time of Jesus, most people walked everywhere, wearing sandals, and shared the same dirty, dusty roads that other people and animals shared. So a person's feet always had a lot more dirt and "nature" on them than our feet generally do now!

The book of Philippians says,

> ⁵Let this mind be in you which was also in
> Christ Jesus, ⁶who, being in the form of God,

did not consider it robbery to be equal with God, ⁷but made Himself of no reputation, taking the form of a bondservant, *and* coming in the likeness of men. ⁸And being found in appearance as a man, He humbled Himself and became obedient to *the point of* death, even the death of the cross. ⁹Therefore God also has highly exalted Him and given Him the name which is above every name, ¹⁰that at the name of Jesus every knee should bow, of those in heaven, and of those on earth, and of those under the earth, ¹¹and *that* every tongue should confess that Jesus Christ *is* Lord, to the glory of God the Father. (Philippians 2:5-11)

The book of Luke contains one of my favorite passages and also provides a wonderful example of the attractiveness of humbleness.

⁷So He told a parable to those who were invited, when He noted how they chose the best places, saying to them: ⁸"When you are invited by anyone to a wedding feast, do not sit down in the best place, lest one more honorable than you be invited by him; ⁹and he who invited you and him come and say to you, 'Give place to this man,' and then you begin with shame to take the lowest place. ¹⁰But when you are invited, go and sit down in the lowest place, so that when he who invited you comes he may say to you, 'Friend, go up higher.' Then you will have glory in the presence of those who sit at

the table with you. [11]For whoever exalts himself will be humbled, and he who humbles himself will be exalted." (Luke 14:7-11)

As any person who has been in leadership for more than just a few years has learned, a genuinely humble leader deflects praise from himself or herself and points it toward the team of subordinates who actually did the work. Conversely, if the mission fails and fingers are being pointed in criticism, the humble—and most effective—leader steps in front of the team of subordinates and takes those arrows of criticism straight into his or her own chest.

The man known as the "American Sniper," the late navy SEAL Chris Kyle, shared some very relevant thoughts about humbleness and the importance of senior leaders, either military or civilian, having the ability to not think more highly of themselves than they ought to. Chris Kyle left the navy and his career as a SEAL with the rank of chief petty officer (E7) after ten years of active duty and four extremely dangerous and violent deployments to Iraq. As a trained sniper, he was credited with 160 kills, the most confirmed enemy kills of any American military sniper. However, it's reported his *unconfirmed* enemy kills were upward of 250.

Chief Kyle relates in his number-one *New York Times* bestselling book *American Sniper* (2012) that in training and during the initial period of time in new units, there was no distinction in how officers and enlisted SEAL candidates were treated. In general, the separation between officers and enlisted personnel in the military is similar to the difference between white collar personnel and blue collar personnel in the civilian sector. Said another way, officers are management (hopefully leaders), and enlisted personnel are the worker bees. When enlisted personnel become more senior in rank, the dividing line between blue collar and white collar is softened, but the distinction between officer and enlisted remains.

Chief Kyle tells how they received some new SEALS to his platoon in Iraq and promptly welcomed them with a little mild-mannered hazing. The new SEALS had graduated training but hadn't yet been assigned to a platoon or experienced combat.

> The idea was to give them a little exposure to war, a little taste of what they were getting into before they trained up for the main event. We were pretty careful with them—we didn't allow them to go out on ops. Being SEALs, they were chomping at the bit, but we held them back, treating them like gofers at first: Hey, go line up the Hummers so we can go. It was a protection thing; after all we'd just been through (one SEAL killed, another severely injured), we didn't want them getting hurt out in the field.
>
> We did have to haze them, of course. This one poor fella, we shaved his head and his eyebrows, then spray-glued the hair back on his face.
>
> While we were in the middle of doing that, another new guy walked into the outer room.
>
> "You don't want to go in there," warned one of our officers.
>
> The new guy peeked in and saw his buddy getting pummeled.
>
> "I gotta."
>
> "You don't want to go in there," repeated the officer. "It's not going to end well."

"I have to. He's my buddy."

"Your funeral," said the officer, or words to that effect.

New guy number two ran into the room. We respected the fact that he was coming to his friend's rescue, and showered him with affection. Then we shaved him too, taped them together, and stood them in the corner.

Just for a few minutes. (Kyle, 330)

Chief Kyle goes on to say that they also razzed a new officer who didn't take it well at all; he didn't like being manhandled by enlisted men. When a new SEAL first reports to a SEAL team, he is again new and subject to hazing. Chief Kyle says that most officers take it well, but that there are exceptions. He also said that the hazing helps the rest of the SEALs learn and remember who are the better team players and perhaps more likely to respond best in combat situations. He asks, "who do you want on your back, the guy who ran in to save his buddy [from hazing] or the officer who shed tears because he was mistreated by some dirty enlisted men." According to Chief Kyle, the hazing humbles all the new guys, officer and enlisted. He concludes by saying, "I've had good officers, but all of the great ones were humble" (Kyle, 332).

Marine, the Life of Chesty Puller is a biography about Marine Lieutenant General Chesty Puller, written by Burke Davis. Lieutenant General Puller is widely considered to be one of the greatest battlefield commanders in American history. He was universally admired and respected by his men because of his brilliant tactical intuitiveness, his workhorse mentality, his humbleness, and that he treated the enlisted marines with respect.

In 1917 he entered the Virginia Military Institute. He had an average year during his freshman, or "Rat" year, but decided to quit at the end of the year because he felt he couldn't wait to get into the war (World War I). He thought enlisting in the marines was the quickest way to get into the war, and he could then become a commissioned officer in the marines. His humble foundations as a young man and then enlisting in the marines gave him great appreciation for hard work and mental and physical toughness (Davis, 15).

Not only did Lieutenant General Puller exude humbleness in his own character, he disdained pride or haughtiness exhibited by officers under his command. In one example, then Colonel Puller was walking on post one day when he came upon a private at rigid attention and saluting a nearby lieutenant [the most junior officer grade] over and over, like a robot. The lieutenant stood with his hands on his hips watching the private and had a superior air about him. When Colonel Puller asked what was happening, the lieutenant said, "This marine, sir, he neglected to salute me as we passed, and I've ordered him to salute one hundred times."

Colonel Puller answered, "You're right, Lieutenant. So right. But you know that an officer must return every salute he receives. Now let me see you get to it, and do your share" (Davis, 101). So through Colonel Puller's wise leadership and a lesson on humbleness to all who witnessed the scene, the lieutenant became a victim of his own prideful behavior!

As a cadet at USAFA and then as a junior officer in the air force, I always took notice of how more senior officers responded to my crisp salutes that I put significant effort into making technically correct. I appreciated the officers who smiled or even responded with a kind greeting. Likewise, if they just returned the salute with a blank face or even a scowl, I certainly took note and may have even grumbled a less than kind greeting under my breath. That's why, from day one as a

2nd lieutenant on May 29, 1991, I returned every salute with a smile and a heartfelt, "Thank you." Over twenty-three years, that philosophy equated to literally thousands of salutes and thousands of smiles and thank-you's in response. Yes, I know that enlisted people and officers are required to salute those officers that are more senior in rank, but that doesn't mean the senior officer has to make it a laborious job or enforce a reminder that the saluting person is inferior in rank. There is no reason a senior officer cannot be kind and thankful to the junior person for upholding military tradition with a sharp salute and a thank you in return. I don't know if any junior folks ever really appreciated my words of thankfulness, but for me, it was simply the right thing to do. I add this anecdote to encourage you to think about ways you can be a better, more professional, and more humble leader in every aspect.

Being appreciative of and responsive to the customs and courtesies being provided to you by junior professionals (military or civilian) is one way you can be more professional and be humbler. I also believe humble leaders develop humble subordinates. Remember, humbleness does not equate to weakness. History provides thousands of examples of humble, but tough as nails champions and leaders.

Another great example of Chesty Puller teaching humbleness took place in April 1944 at a rest camp on the island of Pavuvu in the Russell Islands. Colonel Puller's men had rigged a crude shower out of a barrel mounted over a canvas shed. The shower water supply had to be filled by bucket from a water source located well down the mountainside.

> Men climbed the hill to wash up after hours
> of working in the black muck, and because of
> the long uphill carry, limited themselves to a

bucket or two of water [from the shower]. Col Puller kept a close watch on the shower. One afternoon as he played cribbage with another Marine, a freshly arrived lieutenant swaggered up the hill with a towel and stiffly starched khakis over his arm. The boy officer kept the shower running far beyond the limit; when he reappeared, Col Puller beckoned:

"Lieutenant, you enjoyed your shower?"

"Yes sir, Colonel. Great!"

"That's grand. Lieutenant, how do you suppose that water gets up there into that barrel?"

"I never thought of that, sir."

"This is your chance, Lieutenant. Every drop of water passes up this hill on the backs of enlisted men. Now you grab those two cans over there and see what you can do about it, Lieutenant."

"Yes, sir."

"And don't let me see you stop for one minute until that barrel is full."

Col. Puller and his cribbage partner played cribbage far into the night, but the paymaster's [Colonel Puller's cribbage partner] mind was not on the game: "That poor, silly kid labored up and down that hill all night, so far as I know. He was still going when we gave up on cribbage." (Davis, 184–185)

I'm sure the saluting lieutenant and the water-carrying lieutenant never forgot Colonel Puller's lessons on humbleness for the rest of their lives!

Later during WWII, then Colonel Puller was the regiment commander of the First Marines.

> Gen Oliver Smith, the assistant division commander, came to observe Puller's work, arrived when Lewis [Colonel Puller] was off on a command post [CP] exercise, simulating an assault landing. Puller, taking only his staff and communications troops of the regiment, had crossed a bay near their camp to land on the far shore. Smith followed in search of Puller, he went in the beach on foot and soon found the command post of the two assault battalions, where their officers awaited developments. Puller was not to be seen. "He's up ahead," an officer said. Smith trudged inland. When he overtook Chesty, Smith laughed: "Lewis, don't you know that by the book you've got to have the regimental CP *behind* the battalion posts?"
>
> "That's not the way I operate," Puller said. "If I'm not up here, my people will say, 'Where on earth is Puller?'"
>
> When Smith had gone, Puller spoke to his staff: "I know you'll hear 'em say I'm a fool for exposing myself, and running along the front lines, and that I'm just a platoon leader at heart. I go up there because that's the only way a field commander can handle a force in combat. It was the reason Lee and Jackson exposed themselves so often in the War Between the States. I recommend it to you. It has nothing to do with

bravery. I can feel fear as much as the next man. I just try to keep my mind on doing my duty."

A young officer spoke up: "But Colonel, you expose yourself like a private, and you're the most valuable man in the outfit."

"No officer's life is worth more than that of any man in his ranks," Puller said. "He may have more effect on the fighting, but if he does his duty, so far as I can see, he must be up front to see what is actually going on with his troops. They'd find a replacement for me soon enough if I got hit. I've never yet seen a Marine outfit fall apart for lack of any one man." (Davis, 186)

In yet another story of Chesty Puller's selflessness and humbleness, Mr. Burke writes that in the Korean War, Colonel Puller was making a check of his marines during the bitter cold winter. Lieutenant Joe Fisher of Item Company reported his men short two parkas, and within a few hours, a runner brought two of the heavy jackets. One of these bore the name, "L. B. Puller," and the other that of Rickert, his executive officer.

Major Don Ezell, walking through the regimental area, saw another young marine with a parka bearing Puller's name, Ezell stopped him.

"What're you doing with that parka, son?"
"Colonel Puller gave it to me."
"Yeah?"
"Sure did. He took it right off when he passed me, and said by God I needed it more than

he did. He wouldn't have it no other way."
(Davis, 276)

How's that for humbleness and putting your subordinates' needs above your own? Colonel Puller, already legendary among marines, knew his men needed a warm parka more than he did, so he gave his parkas to them...pure and simple. Great leaders have the ability to turn their "lens" of how they view themselves and how they view the world, and put others' needs above their own.

This is a great place to add a statement about my strong endorsement of and strong support of good old fashioned Servant Leadership. You are likely familiar with servant leadership and the philosophy that all great leaders truly seek to serve those who they lead. Our job as servant leaders is to seek out the obstacles that have been put in the way, perhaps obstacles even we ourselves have placed in the way, and remove them for our people. A true servant leader understands the privilege and blessing it is to lead, train, shape, and motivate those people under his/her care and authority. Colonel Puller exhibited a great model of servant leadership years before we put a name to it and sold millions of dollars of books about it as if servant leadership was a new way of leading! I'll also again point to Jesus and the example I cited earlier in this chapter about Jesus washing the disciple's feet after the Last Supper. Please remember, the Last Supper took place the night Jesus would be betrayed by his friend and disciple, Judas Iscariot (of course this was all in God's plan and no surprise to Jesus), and then put to death for our sins in the most heinous way the Romans could use at that time, crucifixion. So on that night when He knew He would die the next day with the blackness of our sins (past, present and future) on His shoulders, His thoughts were to teach His disciples how to serve one another and humanity, just as He had done for them. Yes, later in the Garden of Gethsemane He did have a hard time with the impending pain and separation from God the Father He would endure, but He went to the Cross freely, serving His Father and humanity until He breathed His last breath. This is the entire story from John 13:1-17.

> [1]Now before the Feast of the Passover, when Jesus knew that His hour had come that He should depart from this world to the Father, having loved His own who were in the world, He loved them to the end. [2]And supper being ended, the devil having already put it into the heart of Judas Iscariot, Simon's *son,* to betray Him, [3]Jesus, knowing that the Father had given all things into His hands, and that He had come from God and was going to God, [4]rose from supper and laid aside His garments, took a towel and girded Himself. [5]After that, He poured water into a basin and began to wash the disciples' feet, and to wipe *them* with the towel with which He was girded. [6]Then He came to Simon Peter. And *Peter* said to Him, "Lord, are You washing my feet?" [7]Jesus answered and said to him, "What I am doing you do not understand now, but you will know after this." [8]Peter said to Him, "You shall never wash my feet!" Jesus answered him, "If I do not wash you, you have no part with Me." [9]Simon Peter said to Him, "Lord, not my feet only, but also *my* hands and *my* head!" [10]Jesus said to him,

"He who is bathed needs only to wash *his* feet, but is completely clean; and you are clean, but not all of you." [11]For He knew who would betray Him; therefore He said, "You are not all clean." [12]So when He had washed their feet, taken His garments, and sat down again, He said to them, "Do you know what I have done to you? [13]You call Me Teacher and Lord, and you say well, for *so* I am. [14]If I then, *your* Lord and Teacher, have washed your feet, you also ought to wash one another's feet. [15]For I have given you an example, that you should do as I have done to you. [16]Most assuredly, I say to you, a servant is not greater than his master; nor is he who is sent greater than he who sent him. [17]If you know these things, blessed are you if you do them. (John 13:1-17)

I'll bet that if you know or have heard anything about General George S. Patton Jr. previous to my words about him earlier in this book, the word "humble" probably wouldn't come to your mind if asked to describe him. In the book I referenced earlier, *Patten's Principles* (1979), Porter Williamson explains that General Patton was, in fact, very humble in many ways. One of Patton's principles is, "Any man who thinks he is indispensable ain't." I'll quote directly, so you can get the full effect of his wisdom and humbleness.

Gen. Patton did not use "ain't" in his usual conversation. "Ain't" seemed to make this principle strike with greater speed, especially when seasoned with profanity. Gen. Patton would explain, "In war every man is expendable, that includes me, especially me! Any man who starts thinking he is indispensable already isn't worth his weight in anything. I will get rid of such an officer immediately. Every man must be willing to give his life for others to accomplish a mission..."

He would continue, "Any man who starts thinking he is indispensable will start staying from the front. He will spend more time in the rear echelons thinking he is too important to risk his life at the front where the shells are falling. That man is a double coward or a coward twice over. He is afraid of himself and of the enemy. In war every man is expendable."

Gen. Patton transferred officers because of their over-estimation of their importance. I remember one officer who qualified for a transfer in a few short minutes. In the desert [Mojave Desert, pre-WWII training site] we had a two-hour break during the hottest time of the day. Our mail would arrive during this extremely hot period. Usually only one junior officer would walk in the sun to pick up the mail for all of the staff. One day a captain announced that he was going to the mail room and a dozen officers asked to have their mail returned. The captain never returned with the mail! Later, in the mess tent we asked the captain what happened to our mail.

The captain, speaking as seriously as a minister announcing a death, said, "Gentlemen, when I picked up my mail I found my letter of promotion to the rank of Major. I did not deem it proper for a field grade officer to be carrying mail for junior grade officers."

We were so shocked we could not laugh! It was too crazy to believe. Just as Gen. Patton had advised, "Any man who thinks he is so all-important already isn't." This officer lost all of his value for the I Armored Corps the instant he received his promotion.

As our I Armored Corps and Desert Training Center grew in numbers, our staff became more specialized in duties. Every officer had a specific responsibility and the proper amount of authority to get the job done. In addition, we were supposed to know about the activities of all the other sections. This sharing of information was the principal reason for many of our staff meetings.

Gen. Patton would advise, "We can expect that some of us will be killed. We do not want the loss of one man to stop our killing the enemy. Always have a man trained and ready to take over in case you are killed. The test of your success is whether you could be killed and nothing would be lost!"

In civilian life this principle of being humble and teaching humbleness is not followed too frequently. Many corporate executives all the way down the line to the janitors strive to prove their worth by trying to be indispensable. It is a type of job security to keep others from knowing the work operation. Gen. Patton demanded that every man be expendable to win every battle. He did not spare himself. He repeated so often, "I do not know of a better way to die than to be facing the enemy. I pray that I will fall forward when I am shot. That way I can keep firing my pistols! I was shot in the behind in World War I! I do not want to be hit there again. I got a medal for charging at the enemy, but I have had to spend a lot of time explaining how I got shot in the behind! I want to fall forward!" (Williamson, 42–43)

Humbleness can also play a critical role in building relationships, which is also an integral leadership skill. I spent ten years out of my twenty-three years in the air force living in San Antonio, on two separate assignments. I grew to love the small-town feeling of San Antonio. I also loved the weather and the lower cost of living. But I really became enamored with the San Antonio Spurs. In February of 2015, Coach Gregg Popovich won his one thousandth National Basketball Association (NBA) basketball game. Coach Popovich is only the ninth NBA coach in history to win a thousand games. Along with five NBA championship titles with the Spurs, Coach Popovich has won three NBA Coach of the Year honors. I'm not an over-the-top sports fanatic, but I love the way the Spurs play team basketball. I also love the way Coach Popovich demands that his players be people of integrity, character, and humbleness. Legendary basketball player and philanthropist David Robinson was fairly new to the team when I moved to San Antonio in 1991. I very much appreciated David Robinson for many reasons; he was an extremely intelligent graduate of the US Naval Academy, an outstanding basketball player, and a Christian man of character and integrity.

A few years after David Robinson joined the team, Gregg Popovich became the head coach. Coach Pop is a 1975 Air Force Academy graduate, so I liked him for that reason also. Coach Popovich leads his team like a skilled military commander. Over the years, the Spurs also added a few more world-class players like Tim Duncan, Tony Parker, Manu Ginobili, and recently, Kawhi Leonard. Since Coach Pop became the head coach, the Spurs have won those five NBA championships, and the team is widely recognized as the classiest, humblest, and most community-centric team in all professional sports. True, the Spurs have been blessed and fortunate to have NBA Hall of Fame caliber players, but Gregg Popovich is the leader who has created the culture of humble excellence in which the team lives and plays.

Mr. Michael Lee Stallard wrote an online article about why he feels Coach Popovich has been so incredibly successful. He thinks that Coach Popovich creates a culture that produces sustainable superior performance through a series of four factors. Mr. Stallard says that Coach Popovich is intentional about connecting with players and staff to develop relationship excellence. Coach Popovich says, "We are disciplined... but that's not enough. Relationships with people are what it's all about. You have to make players realize you care about them. And they have to care about each other and be interested in each other" (Stallard, 2015).

He works very hard to recruit players who are selfless and who value teamwork. If you watch team operations closely, you will see that the Spurs are quick to trade any players who don't put the team above their own egos and desires.

Coach Pop also cares for players and staff as people, not

just business associates. Coach Popovich cultivates relationship excellence by maintaining an attitude of valuing players and staff as people, rather than thinking of them as means to an end. He invests the time to get to know them. He's interested in their lives outside of basketball. Tim Duncan says, "He's been like a father figure to me. He cares for us not only on a coaching level, but on a personal level, and to have someone like that in your corner means a whole lot. Point guard Tony Parker adds, "it's not just about basketball. And it's very rare in our business to have somebody like that" (Stallard, 2015).

Coach Popovich wouldn't have it any other way, stating, "You can only get so much satisfaction out of the ball going through the hoop. There's gotta be more, and because... they let me get involved in their lives, it's a real joy for me" (Stallard, 2015).

Gregg Popovich has built a culture that has the character strengths of honesty and open-mindedness. He is known for saying exactly what he thinks, complimentary or not so complimentary. He expects and respects candor in his players and staff. They know he wants to hear their opinions and ideas. Coach Popovich's open-mindedness allows him to consider the ideas and opinions of others. This creates an environment that encourages frequent conversations to identify the best solutions. Once Coach Pop believes he has sufficient information to make a good decision, he makes it, and the team moves on.

Lastly, Mr. Stallard says that Coach Popovich has a passion for task excellence. He claims that watching the Spurs play is like watching the basketball equivalent of a Swiss watch. The precision movements, speed, and coordination of the Spurs players is beautiful to behold. Coach Popovich understands that without relationship excellence, task excellence and superior results are built on feet of clay [easily breakable]. Because he intentionally develops relationship excellence among the team, the Spurs are able to achieve task excellence and sustainable, superior performance.

Five NBA championships prove that Coach Gregg Popovich has cultivated a culture that produces sustainable superior performance by developing both relationship excellence and task excellence. Coach Popovich and the Spurs have created a culture of connection that makes players and staff members want to give their best efforts (Stallard, 2015).

There's an excellent quote that I've heard many times regarding humbleness: "Humbleness is not about thinking less of yourself; it is about thinking of yourself less!" This is a perfect way to describe humble leadership. Being humble does not mean you are not confident. Confidence is a very important trait to possess as a leader. Coach Gregg Popovich is this kind of leader. A leader needs to feel like he or she has important skills and knowledge the subordinates need to know. A leader shouldn't think he or she is not worthy of leadership or think he or she lacks qualifications. A humble leader simply needs to keep the focus of the mission and the welfare of his or her people in the front of their mind. The leader's focus should not be on how to get promoted but on how the team can accomplish the mission and how the team can get promoted!

Think about the many athlete interviews you have likely heard throughout your life. You may have heard an athlete say, "I did great. I hit every shot, and I defended like a warrior. I was awesome tonight, and I carried the team on my shoulders." Conversely, you may have heard the athlete who did as well or better than the first who says, "We had a great night. Our team worked very well together, and the crowd gave us great energy. We were just plain blessed, and we will work hard to continue playing well for our fans." Who do you tend to like better, and who makes you feel better about humanity in general? I know for me, the humble athlete wins hands-down every single time. I hate to sound negative, and I don't dislike very many people, but I really dislike the behavior of conceited and egotistic athletes, actors, coaches, and arrogant people in general. I just don't like to be around people like that!

Examine your own speech patterns. How often do you say, "I," in a discussion? Look for all the areas you can to replace "I" with "you," "we," or "our team." I believe you will truly notice your focus shifting to how you can honor and uplift others with your speech. Best part, people around you will notice that you talk in "team-speak" and will gravitate toward you and desire to be a contributing member of your team.

CHAPTER 6
PREPAREDNESS/HARD WORK

The key is not the will to win... everybody has that.
It is the will to prepare to win that is important.
—Bobby Knight, retired college men's basketball
coach, three-time NCAA champion

The largest slug line in Stafford, Virginia, is in a huge park-and-ride lot across the street from a Lowe's and a strip mall. Each work morning, I parked my truck and hurriedly got into line to wait my turn for Rosslyn, Virginia. It's funny to watch people "race-walk" to beat each other into line. They look like the race-walkers we see on TV, hips swaying and arms pumping! But with the idiosyncrasies of slugging, just one additional person ahead of you could mean the difference between a five-minute wait or a twenty-minute wait! One morning I had jumped out of my truck and casually race-walked to the line. Of course, after waiting about ten minutes in line, the sky opened up and rained cats and dogs!

I kept an umbrella in my truck, but with it not raining when I got out of my truck, I had not grabbed it. Now I had the terrible dilemma of deciding if I should get out of line to retrieve my umbrella and lose who knows how much time in getting picked up, or just stand in the rain, hoping it would end soon (hope is *never* a great plan, by the way). I was woefully unprepared for the rain! There were some wonderfully kind slugs in the line who had umbrellas and offered to share, but it's difficult, at best, to share an umbrella with a man who is six foot eight inches tall! So there I stood, getting soaked, but sticking by my plan of...hope!

I also learned the importance of preparing myself for the cold winter days by wearing long johns under my 100 percent polyester, 100 percent cold, blue air force slacks. Of course, wearing long johns in the office was much too warm, so I had to take them off and carry them home in my man purse in the afternoon. Also, for some ridiculous reason, I really disliked the look of earmuffs, especially with a military uniform. I thought they looked silly, and frankly, I thought they looked very wimpy. Well, after often starting the workday with a headache resulting from an earache from the freezing cold, I got over my vainness and started carrying an "Air Force-Approved" set of earmuffs in my man purse! It really was nice to start the day without a headache or earache.

Of imminently more importance than being prepared for the slug line is being prepared for the responsibilities of a leadership position. Sadly, a lot of leaders put about as much thought into their leadership style as I had put into deciding if I needed an umbrella that cold and rainy morning! Preparation for successfully holding leadership positions comes in many forms, be it the environment the leader grew up in, education and other mental training, physical conditioning, and even logistical preparation. Unfortunately, in the military and public service occupations (police, emergency response technicians, and community emergency response offices), a failure to properly prepare for successful leadership may very well result in the death of military teammates, hospital patients, and civilians.

As I wrote at the beginning of this book, I do not believe all great leaders are born leaders. I believe some people by nature may be predisposed toward more successful leadership skill, but I also believe *all* people can learn common successful leadership traits and implement them into their personalities. There are more ways to educate oneself about leadership than ever before in history. There are books, movies, seminars, magazine articles, leadership coaches, and workplace leadership training programs. Many American colleges and universities even offer entire degree programs with leadership as the primary focus. The index of the sources I used for this book is a wonderful guide to just a few of the books I've read about leadership, which, of course, are less than one-tenth of one percent of all leadership books that have ever been written. With today's easy access to technology for virtually every person in every socioeconomic stratum, there are literally thousands of ways to access educational material about leadership.

Since God first created the world, everyone who has ever accomplished something truly great spent significant time preparing their minds, bodies, and spirits for the task ahead of them. Jesus Christ Himself spent approximately thirty years preparing for His ministry, crucifixion, and resurrection. Every two years, the world is treated to the thousands of stories of extreme dedication and preparation that summer and winter Olympians have dedicated to their sport. Most Olympians have spent much of their lives training for their sports. They practiced before school, trained after school, and competed on weekends. They were dedicated to nothing but their sport day after day, month after month, and year after year.

Likewise, medical professionals also spend years and years in education and clinical rotations to earn the right to provide actual hands-on patient care. Surgeons spend four to five years earning a bachelor's degree, four years of medical school, and then five years in a surgical residency just to become a "rookie surgeon." It will be several more years and hundreds of surgeries later before they can be considered an experienced surgeon.

US military professionals are also no strangers to long-term preparation in perfecting their skills in defending the United States. US Navy SEALs spend up to eighteen months in some of the most arduous physical and mentally demanding training that exists in the entire world to wear the famed Trident, signifying them as a SEAL. At that point, new SEALs still spend months and years in highly specialized training to hone their skills and learn new techniques and weaponry.

Medal of Honor recipient and Navy SEAL Lieutenant Michael P. Murphy, who I previously wrote about, showed incredible discipline and persistence in preparing for the Navy SEAL physical entrance exam. In 2001 the SEAL physical screening test consisted of

1. A five-hundred-yard swim using the breaststroke or sidestroke in 12:30
2. A minimum of forty-two push-ups in two minutes
3. A minimum of fifty sit-ups in two minutes
4. A minimum of six dead-hang pull-ups
5. A mile-and-a-half run in 11:30 wearing combat boots and long pants. (Williams, 61)

If we are being honest with ourselves, completing the above tasks in sequence, even with no time constraints, sounds like a pure nightmare. Please remember the above requirements are only the minimums; any successful SEAL candidate scores well above these minimum requirements.

In 1994 a navy captain founded the SEAL Recruiting District Assistance Council (RDAC) to help train potential SEAL candidates. The pass rate for SEAL basic underwater demolition/SEAL (BUD/S) training is a very low 25 percent. The training also costs about $500,000 for a candidate to fully make it through SEAL training. RDAC was developed to help prepare future candidates and to help weed out those interested in becoming a SEAL but may not have the fortitude to make it all the way through training and receive the Trident. RDAC consists of physical screening tests (PST), mentoring sessions, and encouragement both mentally and physically for the demanding BUD/S training.

Lieutenant Murphy participated in the RDAC program. Beginning in January 1998, Lieutenant Murphy took the practice PST five times over the first six months of the year in his ultimately successful attempt just to build a strong application package for BUD/S (Williams, 44–49).

Lieutenant Murphy and thousands of other SEALs, US Air Force pararescuemen, US Air Force combat controllers, Army Delta Force, Army Rangers, Marine Raiders, and other highly trained military professionals work and train harder than the average person can ever conceive of training. The more I've learned about America's Special Operations Forces professionals, the more I stand in awe of their mental and physical strength, dedication, and commitment to the defense of America and its citizens.

Colonel Bud Day also exhibited an enormous ability to think ahead, take advantage of every opportunity, and prepare as thoroughly as possible. As a youth, he worked at a golf course in Sioux City, Iowa, "on the right side of the tracks," and soon deduced that the men playing golf, driving fancy cars, and dressing nicely had all been educated to a higher level than the people he usually interacted with from his home on the "wrong" side of the tracks. He began reading voraciously. He read anything he could get his hands on and developed a penchant for very mature reading. He soon left the world of authors of preteen and teenage books for authors such as Nathan Hale, Thomas Paine, Daniel Webster, Thomas Jefferson, and his favorite, Charles Lindbergh (Coram, 20).

After WWII, the US government paid for a month of college for every month a veteran served on active duty. Colonel Day had earned four years of educational credits from his service in the marines (Coram, 49). He was discharged in 1945 after WWII. He had wanted to become a doctor, but thousands of service members who were medics in the war had returned home and were filling up medical school programs, so he pursued his second career choice of being a lawyer (Coram, 46). Being a lawyer required seven years of school between a bachelor program and law school. Since Colonel Day only had four years of eligibility, he decided he would have to double up his coursework. By 1950 he had graduated with a bachelor's degree from Morningside College in Iowa and had a law school degree from the University of South Dakota (Coram, 57).

He joined the Air Force Reserves in 1950 and came on active duty in 1951 (Coram, 61). In time, Colonel Day was selected for the pilot's school training he volunteered for and graduated in 1952 (Coram, 69). As a pilot, he volunteered for every additional training or certificate he could. He was soon one of the few instrument-trained pilots in the air force, able to fly in zero-visibility weather by relying only on the plane's instruments (Coram, 70). His training and ability to write in a scholarly manner put him in a position to write dozens of air force doctrine manuals for aircraft he had flown. During what many considered to be a dead-end job as a reserve officer training cadet instructor, he went back to school and took classes for a master's degree in international law (Coram, 102).

As a POW, Colonel Day was able to think through leadership challenges, develop the POW command chain structure, and devise ways to communicate. After he retired from the air force and became a private practice lawyer in Florida, his knowledge and leadership skills enabled him to bring a case against the federal government when the Clinton administration discontinued health care to military retirees within military hospitals and clinics. Through many years of dogged preparation, determination, and leadership, he won the case and restored approximately 95 percent of retiree health benefits (Coram, 366). Any military retiree can thank Colonel Bud Day for the health-care benefits we currently receive. And we hope and pray military retiree health-care benefits can withstand any other efforts to diminish them!

By the time most of us are ten years old, we've heard the phases, "poor preparation makes poor performance," or, "practice makes perfect." Preparation and then execution are truly the engines that power performance, productivity, and success in life. If we truly have a goal in our minds, preparation to achieve them is the only way we will ever accomplish those lofty goals each of us dream about. So please keep your hope alive, but remember that hope is not a plan that will help you accomplish your goals. Hoping we will win the Powerball lottery next time it breaks a billion dollars, or hoping that perfect job will fall into our laps even though we are unqualified for it, will probably not happen for most of us! Action through preparedness will keep you slugging toward the goals you have set for yourself, your family, and your business. Remember also to give your hopes, goals, and ambitions over to the Lord in addition to the actions you will take. Then you can step back and prepare to be amazed at what He will do!

As important as preparedness is, we, of course, need to follow through on all that preparedness and put it into action! You've seen my earlier references to the value of plain old hard work. You've probably heard thousands of success stories where the person would not have obtained that success without, "always being the hardest working person in the room," as I quoted Dwayne Johnson earlier. As mature adults interested in improving your leadership skills, you already know the times in your life where you've been very successful were possible only because of the blood, sweat, and tears you put into that particular effort.

Those of you who watched professional football during the 1970s remember Rocky Bleier of the Pittsburgh Steelers. He was a tough as nails running back who worked very hard every game and "left it out there on the field" at the end of every game. His success story is simply amazing and a tremendous testament to hard work and persistence. He had been a soldier in Vietnam and severely injured by a grenade blast. His legs were riddled with shrapnel to the extent that he couldn't walk. He even lost part of a foot due to the damage. He spent agonizing months pushing his body to the full limit just to learn how to walk again. But that wasn't enough. He kept pushing and working until he could run. Then he pushed more and regained the running skills he had before his injury. His unfathomable hard work was rewarded by earning his way back to the Steelers, becoming a star running back, and winning several Super Bowl rings!

Being a successful leader is the same way; we can't just do it half-heartedly. Your people need to know you have their backs. They need to know you have the integrity, knowledge, and toughness to lead them through whatever mission you are on together.

Of course, as we all know, your drive for leadership and success *must* be balanced with your family, spiritual, physical, and emotional needs. A person simply cannot spend all his or her time at work and neglect the beautiful family the Lord has given you. Being a father or mother to those children is *the* most important leadership role you will ever have. Failure as a leader in your family (and sufficient time is a requirement) cannot be an option; you and your family must succeed!

CHAPTER 7

PATIENCE

Having longsuffering patience is definitely a characteristic a slug must possess—or soon learn—if they want to be part of the undulating slug movement. As stated previously, the slugging-window, depending on how far away you live from where you work in DC/VA, is about an hour. In my case, in Stafford, Virginia, the slug-lot is usually active from 5:30 a.m. to 6:45 a.m. The chance of being picked up after that diminishes greatly. Also, depending on the location and size of the federal entity or company you work at, there are more drivers for some, fewer drivers for other places. From Stafford, the Pentagon was the most popular destination, then Crystal City (five minutes south of the Pentagon), and then maybe Rosslyn. Rosslyn was not extremely popular, so it was a little tougher for us Rosslyn slugs. I may have waited only five minutes on an extremely lucky day or up to twenty-five minutes on a very slow day. Of course, getting picked up all depends on how many slugs are in line ahead of you and how many drivers there are on any particular day.

In my mind, there are two aspects of patience. We can be patient when it comes to physical time, or we can be patient in dealing with our fellow human beings. Regarding patience about physical time, examples include when we wait patiently at a doctor's office or a forever-long line at Walmart. Chief Petty Officer Chris Kyle wrote about the incredible time and patience required to be skilled sniper. Chief Kyle and other US snipers would often spend several hours or more just reaching [usually crawling] a sniping position in the field. After taking the shot(s), an equal amount of patience was required to successfully leave the position. If the sniper got up and walked, or even crawled away so quickly as to disrupt the landscape, he could draw the enemy's attention and put himself in danger. A hasty retreat could also give away a useful position for future sniping activities (Kyle, 111).

The second aspect of patience I'll discuss is patience with our fellow human beings. What parent hasn't had to learn patience with a child a thousand times over? What worker hasn't had to practice patience with a coworker?

There is the old lighthearted prayer, "God please give me patience, and give it to me now!" How does God usually give us patience, though? He doesn't usually just infiltrate our minds with the gift of patience. Rather, He allows us to be in situations where we can learn to be patient by examining and governing our responses to difficult situations.

The biblical story of Noah building the ark is an incredible story of patience. In the book of Genesis, chapter 6, God tells Noah, "[13]And God said to Noah, "The end of all flesh has come before Me, for the earth is filled with violence through them; and behold, I will destroy them with the earth. [14]Make yourself an ark of gopherwood; make rooms in the ark, and cover it inside and outside with pitch." (Genesis 6:13-14) God goes on to explain the exact dimensions of the ark, who should be on the ark (Noah's wife, three sons, and their wives), and that a male and female of every animal would join them.

Previous to these verses, God said, "³And the LORD said, "My Spirit shall not strive with man forever, for he *is* indeed flesh; yet his days shall be one hundred and twenty years." (Genesis 6:3) God was saying He would send the flood in 120 years. That means Noah and his family worked on building the ark, gathering food, and gathering animals for 120 years! Even in a country that hadn't seen rain, Noah trusted God and patiently worked on the ark for all those years. After entering the ark, most scholars think Noah, his family, and the animals were actually on the ark for close to a year. Noah's patience and faith in the Lord took him through 121 years for God's plan to come to fruition.

The biblical story of the battle of Jericho is another awesome, albeit shorter, example of people exercising patience and being rewarded for it. Joshua chapter 6, says,

> Now Jericho was securely shut up because of the children of Israel; none went out, and none came in. And the Lord said to Joshua: "See! I have given Jericho into your hand, its king, and the mighty men of valor. You shall march around the city, all you men of war; you shall go all around the city once. This you shall do six days. And seven priests shall bear seven trumpets of rams' horns before the Ark [Ark of the Covenant that they carried]. But the seventh day you shall march around the city seven times, and the priests shall blow the trumpets. It shall come to pass, when they make a long blast with the ram's horn, and when you hear the sound of the trumpet, that all the people shall shout with a great shout; then the wall

of the city will fall down flat. And the people shall go up every man straight before him." (Joshua 6:1–5)

So that's exactly what Joshua and the Israelites did, showing incredible patience and discipline. I'll continue in Joshua.

And Joshua rose early in the morning, and the priests took up the Ark of the Lord. Then seven priests bearing seven trumpets of rams' horns before the ark of the Lord went on continually and blew with the trumpets. And the armed men went before them. But the rear guard came after the ark of the Lord, while the priests continued blowing the trumpets. And the second day they marched around the city once and returned to the camp. So they did six days. But it came to pass on the seventh day that they rose early, about the dawning of the day, and marched around the city seven times in the same manner. On that day only they marched around the city seven times. And the seventh time it happened, when the priests blew the trumpets, that Joshua said to the people: "Shout, for the Lord has given you the city! Now the city shall be doomed by the Lord to destruction, it and all who are in it. Only Rahab the harlot shall live [Rahab had helped the Israelites scout the city], she and all who are with her in the house, because she hid the messengers that we sent. And you, by all means abstain from the accursed things, lest you become accursed when you take of the accursed things, and make the camp of Israel a curse, and trouble it. But all the silver and gold, and vessels of bronze and iron, are consecrated to the Lord; they shall come into the treasury of the Lord." So the people shouted when the priests blew the trumpets. And it happened when the people heard the sound of the trumpet, and the people shouted with a great shout, that the wall fell down flat. Then the people went up into the city, every man straight before him, and they took the city. And they utterly destroyed all that was in the city, both man and woman, young and old, ox and sheep and donkey, with the edge of the sword. (Joshua 6:12–21)

God rewarded the Israelites' patience and obedience with a complete and devastatingly successful victory, and He can and will do the same for all of us, if we only let Him.

Just like leadership in general, there are thousands and thousands of books, articles, and online sources of information about the importance of having patience in every leader's toolbox. I'll reference a few sources that focus on the criticality of patience.

The online article "Patience in Leadership: More Discipline than Virtue" lists several advantages practicing patience has for leaders.

1. Patience allows us to suspend judgment long enough to make considered decisions. Instead of making snap or rash decisions, especially when the pressure is on,

practicing patience gives a leader the benefit of stopping to consider the impact of the decisions they make and who/what will be affected by the decision.

2. Patience allows for the development of late bloomers. Each person, regardless of whether they are fast like a rabbit or slower like the tortoise [or slug!], needs solid leadership to help them get to the finish line. Leaders need the patience to guide the rabbit and reach back and encourage the tortoise.

3. Patience can help leaders become better listeners. To get better understanding and build trust and value in relationships, a leader needs to suspend his or her own judgment and focus on what is being said.

4. Patience can help us manage stress. If a leader is frequently impatient with those around them, they are also likely frequently frustrated and possibly angry. Nobody wants to work with or for a person who is perpetually angry and likely to lash out in angry words and actions (Teatro, 2012).

Retired army general Colin Powell, former secretary of state and former chairman of the Joint Chiefs of Staff is highly regarded as one of the finest leaders America has ever produced. One of his "Lessons on Leadership" is, "The day soldiers stop bringing you their problems is the day you have stopped leading them." If people bring you their problems, that is a good thing. When people stop bringing you their problems, it's a sign you've failed them as a leader. When people no longer share their problems, you lose touch with what's going on (JD, 2014).

General Powell focused on listening in this axiom, which I'll also discuss in the next chapter, but extending patience is also a very large part of this lesson on leadership. As stated before, unless a leader patiently listens to problems, allows subordinates to discuss and work through problems in an educational manner, and then implements the fixes to the problems with maturity and patience, that leader will soon fail.

Each of us can likely look back on our lives at hundreds of successes we have had either in academics, in athletics, on the job, or in relationships because we exhibited a certain degree of patience. We wanted success badly enough in that particular area that we were willing to be patient and wait and work for the success we had been pursuing. I understand persistence is closely related to success, but patience is also a critical factor. Conversely, we can look back and say, "If I had only been more patient," we might have accomplished that goal, or more importantly, we wouldn't have failed in that relationship at work or at home.

Anyone reading this book who is in their forties or fifties and watched David Carradine in *Kung Fu* undoubtedly remembers the guidance he received from his master, "Patience, Grasshopper, patience." Well, I say to you, "Patience, slug, patience!" By daily endeavoring to practice patience, a person will absolutely improve his or her life and improve the lives of those at home and at work. And that's a promise!

CHAPTER 8
COMMUNICATION/ACTIVE LISTENING

As stated previously, one of the cardinal rules of slugging is not to talk to the driver, or the other slugs for that matter. However, it was very important to listen closely to what destination the driver calls out when driving by the slug line. If you dally in getting to the car, the next overeager slug (nice oxymoron, huh?) quickly gets into the car!

Who hasn't been accused of being a poor listener? Chances are when we were children, our folks told us we didn't listen well. Of course, that curse has been revisited upon us who are now parents of our own non-listening little miracles! Most of us have also probably been accused of not listening well by spouses, friends, or even bosses. Enough self-critique on us, though. We all have also worked for bosses who simply don't listen to anyone well!

There are many reasons a person may not listen well, as I'll discuss later. But some of the major reasons are that one may be very busy and preoccupied. There may be some situation going on at home that is diverting his or her attention. They may have such strong preconceived ideas about the topic that they simply can't wait for you to be through talking, so they can share their knowledge with you. Lastly and hopefully less often, they may just plain be rude and have never bothered to learn and practice basic courtesy in letting someone else finish a sentence. There are few things more irritating, or hurtful, than somebody who continually cuts you off in midsentence and doesn't let you finish your words.

James Hunter, in *Servant Leader*, expands on the bad habit of people cutting off others when they are talking by proposing the thought that they obviously are not listening very well if they've formulated their opinions and are so impatient to tell you about them that they cut you off. Also, consciously or subconsciously, they don't value the other person or his or her opinion because they can't even take the time to fully hear someone's thoughts. Even if they cut us off subconsciously and respect us on some level, *they* have to align their feelings of respect with actions of respect (Hunter, 49). A husband, wife, father, and mother must align their *feelings* of respect and love with *actions* of respect and love. A leader must also align their *feelings* of respect with *actions* of respect.

Michael Stallard also wrote a great article about how leaders listening to the worker bees (soldiers) in the trenches—literally *in the trenches*—helped America win WWII. He asks a vital question for leaders: "What would happen if you trusted your team members enough to give them the freedom to take risks and voice ideas openly?"

His article goes on to say that some of the ideas you receive will sound crazy. Some will flop. But others will be just what your organization needs to solve an important challenge. One of the most remarkable examples of what can happen when group members are given autonomy and encouraged to voice their ideas occurred during WWII, as recounted by Stephen Ambrose in his book *Citizen Soldiers*.

In June of 1944, after American soldiers landed on the beaches of Normandy on D-Day and moved about ten miles inland, they approached the Normandy countryside the French refer to as the Brocage. This part of France consisted of plots of land that farmers separated with hedgerows rather than fences. The hedgerows were made of two to three feet of packed soil at their bases and topped off with several feet (up to ten to twelve feet) of brush and vines.

When the Sherman tanks attempted to go over the top of the hedgerows, the front of the tank popped up, exposing its thin underbelly to Nazi antitank fire. As it turns out, Allied military planners had spent so much time planning for the D-Day landings that they hadn't fully considered the problems troops might encounter in hedgerow country. The Sherman tanks' vulnerability caught everyone by surprise.

At first, Americans tried blasting the hedgerows open, so the Sherman tanks could then progress through the holes created by the explosions. Unfortunately, the explosions only served to give the Nazis advance warning of where the tanks were going. Nearly a month after D-Day, the Allies were falling behind schedule primarily because of the problems created by the hedgerows and the Nazi defense.

One day in a discussion between officers and the enlisted men, the idea arose of mounting saw-teeth on the front of the Sherman tank. Many of those present laughed at the suggestion. One soldier, however, took the idea seriously. Sergeant Curtis G. Culin, a cab driver from Chicago, immediately designed and built a hedgerow cutting device from pieces of steel the Nazis had strewn across the beaches to slow down an amphibious attack. When tested, the new device easily sliced through the hedgerows.

It wasn't long before the Sherman tanks mounted with Culin's device were branded "Rhinos" by the soldiers because they made a Sherman tank look like a rhinoceros. Within days of testing the Rhinos, the idea was presented to General Omar

Bradley, head of the First Army. In short order, he attended a demonstration of the Rhino tank and immediately ordered five hundred of Culin's devices. Within two weeks, 60 percent of the First Army's Sherman tanks were modified into Rhinos. With the Rhinos, the First Army were able to proceed through the hedgerow country in time to crush the Nazi army.

Curtis Culin's innovation might not have occurred had it not been for a chain of command consisting of Generals Omar Bradley, Dwight D. Eisenhower, and George C. Marshall, each of whom gave the soldiers under his command the freedom to share and test ideas.

As a leader, one of the most powerful things you can do is demonstrate that you are willing to listen. Encourage your team to take the initiative in identifying problems, and give them the freedom to find solutions. By doing so, you just might unleash the type of innovative thinking that allowed a Chicago cab driver to play a crucial role in one of history's greatest moments (Stallard, 2015).

In 2000 I had the opportunity to attend a communication seminar lead by former Texas state senator Judith Zaffirini, PhD. Dr. Zaffirini lists some tips for better listening and some interesting facts.

1. Listening is the key to communicating effectively, not only at the interpersonal level and small group levels, but also at the organizational level. We need to ensure that the message we send is received and that we receive messages intended for us. Remove, or at least minimize, distracting background noise and activities.
2. Americans typically listen four times faster than we speak, so listeners have time to observe nonverbal cues and analyze vocal cues which color the verbal content.

3. Selective exposure, perception, and retention interfere with the ability to listen accurately and to understand intended messages. Discipline yourself accordingly and determine to listen actively, fairly, and openly. Concentrate on intent.
4. Be aware that many listeners block messages that are inconsistent with their beliefs, attitudes, values, and that we seek consistent, reinforcing information.
5. Listening facilitates responding appropriately and engaging in helical interaction. Do not simply wait for our turn to reply or start formulating our answer. Listen actively!
6. When appropriate, take notes while listening. Later review notes; fill in information where needed. The concentration tends to improve listening because it requires concentration, effort, reinforcement, and review.
7. Ask questions to engage in constructive interaction.
8. Send positive, reinforcing messages such as nodding, smiling, laughing, and agreeing.
9. Do not create interpersonal communication barriers: interrupting, finishing a person's sentences, staccato questioning, nonresponsive answers, failure to ask questions to clarify, and lack of vocal variety. (Zaffirini, 11)

Robert Cromer, the CEO of Adcade, suggests leaders should routinely ask themselves these questions.

1. What am I not saying that needs to be said?
2. What am I saying that's not being heard?
3. What's being said that I'm not hearing?

Rudyard Kipling once said, "Words are, of course, the most powerful drug used by mankind." That is an amazing quote!

We've also heard that "Sticks and stones may break my bones, but words will never hurt me." However, as we grow older, we learn the true power of words. We learn that for most people, words have a tremendous impact on their views of the world, of others, or view of themselves. If you allow yourself to truly feel words, you know that a positive statement can lift your thoughts of yourself to new and almost heavenly heights. You also know that a negative comment can bring you down to the deepest depths of the ocean. Even now, I'm sure you can close your eyes and recall a comment that was said to you ten, twenty, or even thirty years ago. You can remember exactly how that comment, either positive or negative, impacted you at that time. You can sense even now how that comment made you feel, as if the sound of those words still echoes through your thoughts. You can remember if you cried tears of sadness or if your heart surged with excitement and thoughts of strength, love, or popularity.

One extremely useful way to communicate and have people remember what you said is through the use of stories. Unfortunately, we as leaders or parents are often so busy that our requests or directives are often too short and too concise. Our requests may even lack a personal touch or a warm sentiment, which is especially important with our children. Again, close your eyes, and think of some stories you have heard through the years and remember to this day. Conversely, we've all forgotten more terse-directives or efficiently written how-to guides than we can count. I also struggle with wanting to just get the information or request transmitted to the intended recipient without making the effort to make the conversation a more pleasant experience for the recipient. I need to remember that recipients will likely remember the conversation much better if I put it into some type of story. According to Mr.

Briner and Mr. Pritchard in *Leadership Lessons of Jesus,* some of the best known effective communicators were great storytellers. They list Aesop, Abraham Lincoln, Mark Twain, Garrison Keillor, President Ronald Reagan, and of course, Jesus Christ.

Mr. Briner and Mr. Pritchard state that "Jesus both established and perfected the use of parables as a leadership methodology. Just think of the heroes He created who continue to inspire us—the Good Samaritan (Luke 10:30–37), the good and faithful servant (Matthew 25:14–29), the wise virgins (Matthew 25:1–13), the poor widow (Mark 12:41–43), and others" (Briner and Pritchard, 47–48).

As leaders, we can enhance our leadership styles and help others remember our lessons (because all leaders should all be teachers, right?) through using tested and true communication techniques. Communication via relevant stories that create heroes, build legends, and help to establish a workplace or home conducive to learning can also inspire our followers to excellence.

Failure to properly communicate is almost 100 percent of the reason for breakdowns in relationships, be they husband and wife, parents and children, or country and another country. In actuality, regardless even of what we aspire to as a leader, communication is so critical to a harmonious society that we *must* make every effort to become the best communicators that we can be.

CHAPTER 9

SITUATIONAL AWARENESS AND ATTENTION TO DETAIL

As I stated previously, under normal circumstances a driver usually needs to pick up two slugs to have the required three passengers for the HOV lane on I-95. I vividly remember standing in the slug line on cold and rainy days near the end of the optimal time when drivers would be coming through to pick up slugs. Often I would see and hear a driver telling the those at the front of the line that he or she would take extra slugs to get them out of the cold and ensure they had a ride. Yes, that gift of kindness may have made it tough for another driver to get the required slugs later, but to those cold and wet slugs who were waiting, that driver was definitely a leader who displayed a strong sense of situational awareness. That driver was a hero!

Slugs also had to display a keen sense of situational awareness. Certain drivers tend to make a name or reputation for themselves over time. There are those who are known to be extremely kind, giving the slugs a warm welcome and asking if they were comfortable with the temperature or radio setting. Conversely, there are those who didn't respond to a greeting when we got into the car. They just gave a rueful look, like they hated having you in their cars and couldn't wait to get you out. Then there were the aggressive drivers who scared the tar out of us slugs! They jammed on the brakes or floored the accelerator with equal gusto, not aware of the beauty of a gradual deceleration or acceleration. Those drivers who cut off other drivers or cussed when someone wasn't going fast enough in front of them made for an unpleasant ride for everyone in the vehicle!

One of the more comical situations was that of the "Woodstock van." There was a white-haired man who was, by conservative estimates, no younger than eighty years old. He drove a blue Dodge minivan with license plates that declared, "Woodstock 69." By all accounts, while being a nice man, he was an awful driver. Seems he couldn't see very well anymore, and speed was of the essence, or maybe some of his chemical experimentation at Woodstock had lingering effects! You could easily hear the audible groans of displeasure when his unmistakable van came around the corner of the slug line and pulled up to the front!

Slugs who knew of drivers they didn't want to ride with would often basically take a "pass" if their turn came up for a ride and a driver they didn't care for was next. Usually, everyone respects the opinions of others, and the process proceeds as a normal and pleasant experience.

Similarly, history is full of anecdotes of leaders who excelled at situational awareness, won the battle for the day, and saved American lives. Sadly, history is also replete with examples of leaders who misread the situation they were in, or didn't try to read it at all, and American lives were lost.

Related to having an acute sense of situational awareness is cultivating a strict sense of attention to detail. Our lives are so controlled by the exacting requirements of technology, machines, rules, and the clock that if we aren't paying very close attention to detail, we are likely to make a significant mistake, sometimes with catastrophic consequences.

Dr. David Gibbs, president of the US-based Christian Law Association, spoke at my church in July 2015. He provided this hilarious anecdote about the importance of paying strict attention to detail. In the early 1970s, Dr. Gibbs and his wife wanted to take a small camping vacation. Still wanting some comforts of home, they rented a small mobile home for the weekend. Dr. Gibbs had never been around or operated a mobile home before, but the young lawyer was full of confidence and felt there was nothing he couldn't figure out, or at least read the directions to decipher what needed to be done.

Dr. Gibbs and his family made it to their vacation site in good shape and were soon enjoying a wonderful respite in Nashville, Tennessee. After about three days of bliss, his wife noticed a red light gleaming from an inside control panel that hadn't been illuminated before. Not knowing what the light meant, Dr. Gibbs quickly did his research and learned that the mobile home's waste-holding tanks needed to be emptied. So after reading the directions and feeling confident about how to empty the tanks, he found the campsite's waste-holding tank emptying site and proceeded to hook up the various tubes from the mobile home into the campsite tank. He had read that when he had everything ready to go, he was to flip a switch on the opposite side of the mobile home that would increase air pressure into the mobile home holding tank, thereby aiding the waste in moving out of the mobile home tank and into the campsite's tank. The amount of air pressure to be applied was a fairly meager 10.5 pounds per square inch (psi). However, in a blatant "fail" in applying attention to detail, Dr. Gibbs misread that the psi required was 105 psi... more than ten times the required pressure inside the mobile home tank!

As Dr. Gibbs and his family were getting everything set to empty the tank, another mobile home pulled up next to him.

This mobile home was the Taj Mahal compared to his small and rudimentary rented mobile home. It was at least four times the length of Dr. Gibbs's home and had fancy paint and mag wheels to match. The windows were open, and upbeat music could be heard blasting inside. The owner jumped out and engaged in conversation with Dr. Gibbs. The owner wasn't at all shy about his status in life and financial means, stating that he had just bought the home for $232,000. Folks, in my mind, that is a ridiculous amount to pay for a mobile home in today's market! I checked online and found that $232,000 in 1975 is roughly the equivalent of $1,025,481 today in 2015! Can you imagine a million-dollar mobile home? The mobile home owner had never used his home before and had actually just stopped by the campground to blow a minute amount of dust out of his immaculate home's waste-holding tanks.

As Dr. Gibbs and the new mobile home owner were talking about the grandeur of the new home, the pressure in Dr. Gibbs's tank had been building continuously until the tank actually became misshapen and looked as if it would explode, but Dr. Gibbs didn't realize the significance of the bloated tank. When he saw that the pressure had built to almost 105 psi, he asked his wife to push and hold the mobile home waste tube down into the campsite hole while he went to the other side to flip the switch that would release the pressure and start the waste flow. On flipping the switch and hearing a giant sucking sound, followed very closely by his wife's blood-curdling screams, he knew he had a "nasty" problem!

He sprinted around the back of his mobile room to find his wife clutching the tube tightly to her chest while the remainder of the tube, about eight feet above her head, blew human waste from the tube with a velocity that made the tube viciously move side to side and all around, just like a balloon that's been filled with air and then released takes off like a rocket and flies in every direction! The closest object to the tube, the Taj Mahal home, took the brunt of the "poo-blast," and the open screened windows on the entire side of the new home easily succumbed to the poo-velocity! Dr. Gibbs's new "friend" didn't escape the poo-torrent either! Needless to say, the two couples did not enjoy supper together that evening! After an abrupt conversation with the Taj Mahal owner and their hasty exit, the Gibbs family later found "evidence" of Dr. Gibbs's inattention to detail in the campsite's kiddy pool, a full 150 feet beyond where the hurricane force devastation had taken place!

I also appreciate this story of General Patton's attention to detail. Of course, I love it even more because it speaks of General Patton's knowledge of the Bible. Mr. Williamson writes in *Patton's Principles* about the story when General Patton supposedly corrected a high-ranking church officer on the proper words of a biblical quotation the church officer had used. The church officer reacted strongly that there was no way that a man as profane as General Patton was could know the Bible well enough to quote any verse, no less correct a church leader on the correct verbiage.

Mr. Williamson says, as the story goes,

> Gen. Patton reacted with the same degree of anger, stating that the head of such a great church should not utter false religious verses. Gen. Patton, to settle the dispute, ordered an attendant to get a Bible. Before the attendant could return Gen. Patton asked the head of the church for the chapter and verse of the quotation which he had attempted to quote.

The church leader could not give neither chapter nor verse, so Gen. Patton walked to the blackboard and wrote the author, chapter and exact verse. Turning to the audience, he recited the verse. The attendant brought the Bible into the room, and Gen. Patton pointed to the blackboard and ordered the attendant to read the cited verse. As the attendant read, it was obvious that Gen. Patton had quoted the verse correctly, and the head of the church was wrong. The church leader's comment was that he had taken the verse out of context. Gen. Patton smiled and said, "The head of a church should never take the Bible out of context!" (Williamson, 64)

As leaders, we have to know the context of what we are supposed to be leading others to do. In my opinion, it's similar to the well-accepted theory that to teach material, the teacher needs to know the material extremely well, so he or she can explain the intricacies of the subject in minute detail and to be able to answer students' questions thoroughly and completely. As leaders, we need to pay strict attention to detail in knowing what our people and the mission need to be successful at any given time. I respectfully ask you to not be the leader who just has a general knowledge of the details of an operation. Be the leader who lives and breathes the details of a mission so that when the going gets tough, you can step out and confidently lead your team to mission success!

CHAPTER 10

THE GOLDEN RULE

At last I offer the secret you have been waiting for. This little-known, easily learned, and easily implemented philosophy is simply the greatest leadership principle ever created, bar none. Yes, it's the biblical concept that we commonly call the Golden Rule. Found in the Bible in the book of Matthew, Jesus advises His listeners to simply, "[12]Therefore, whatever you want men to do to you, do also to them, for this is the Law and the Prophets." (Matthew 7:12). Modern humankind has spent literally billions of hours and billions of dollars in developing, marketing, and disseminating thousands of leadership philosophies. However, I'm saying almighty God gave us all the blueprint we ever needed for exceptional leadership that anybody can learn and implement, over two thousand years ago when Christ was here on earth healing the sick and preaching to the masses.

Let that soak in. You already have all the knowledge, skill, and ability right within your souls to become extremely effective leaders! Now I realize that many would argue and say using the Golden Rule as a leadership philosophy drastically oversimplifies leadership. However, ask yourself the following questions: Do you like to be treated with respect, kindness, patience, and even friendliness? Are you generally more receptive to a leader who treats you with respect in the workplace? Do we want to display respect, kindness, patience, and friendliness? Do we appreciate it when a boss takes the time to know who we are as a person outside the workplace? Do we also want to work in an environment where the leadership has fostered stability, consistency, structure, and fairness, and where education is also seamlessly interwoven into daily activities? Take that stream of thinking farther. Do we as professional men and women also appreciate being challenged in the workplace? And now for the gut-check question. Do we want to be held accountable for our actions and our work performance? If we can honestly answer yes to all of these questions, I submit that the Golden Rule given by the Lord Jesus Christ Himself is not only the greatest rule for how humanity can coexist in love and harmony, it's also the greatest leadership principle ever created.

There are those who would argue that if we treated everyone like we treat ourselves, nothing would ever get done, because we basically don't want to work hard and would rather goof around most of the day. However, if we are serious about our work and conscientious in wanting to actually earn our wages, which I believe most people are, I believe the tenets of the Golden Rule will resonate with us. If we allowed our workers to do whatever they want in the workplace and not work, the company or mission will undoubtedly fail. That is absolutely true. However, I'm implying the belief that people are generally good, honest, ethical, hardworking, and *want* to actually *earn* their salary for the day.

The argument about leading by the Golden Rule brings into the concept of what is a need versus what is a want. Mr. Hunter says in *Servant Leader* that leaders absolutely need to identify and meet the *needs* of their people to serve them most appropriately. Leaders should not identify and meet the *wants* of their people and be slaves to them. Slaves do what others *want*; servants do what others *need*.

By giving into people's wants, a leader is not giving them what they need. Adults, ourselves included, and children need an environment with boundaries. Standards must be set, and people must be held accountable. People may not want boundaries and accountability, but we need boundaries and accountability. A leader should never settle for mediocrity. All people have a need to be pushed—some harder than others—to be the best they can be. It may not be what they, or we, want at that time, but the leader should always be more concerned with needs than wants (Hunter, 65–66).

Of course, Jesus Christ displayed the most incredible display of compassion and treating others as better than Himself by going to the Cross. In addition, the Bible is replete with stories of God and Christ treating others with the greatest of love and compassion. I think of Christ's compassion on the two occasions He fed thousands and thousands of people who sought Him out to hear His authoritative words about the kingdom of God. One instance of Christ feeding thousands is found in Matthew 14:13–21.

> [13]When Jesus heard *it*, He departed from there by boat to a deserted place by Himself. But when the multitudes heard it, they followed Him on foot from the cities. [14]And when Jesus went out He saw a great multitude; and He was moved with compassion for them, and healed their sick. [15]When it was evening, His disciples came to Him, saying, "This is a deserted place,

and the hour is already late. Send the multitudes away, that they may go into the villages and buy themselves food."

[16]But Jesus said to them, "They do not need to go away. You give them something to eat."

[17]And they said to Him, "We have here only five loaves and two fish."

[18]He said, "Bring them here to Me." [19]Then He commanded the multitudes to sit down on the grass. And He took the five loaves and the two fish, and looking up to heaven, He blessed and broke and gave the loaves to the disciples; and the disciples gave to the multitudes. [20]So they all ate and were filled, and they took up twelve baskets full of the fragments that remained. [21]Now those who had eaten were about five thousand men, besides women and children.

Again, that's just one of a hundred examples of Jesus's compassion and kind treatment to others in spite of His own feelings of tiredness, hunger, and even discouragement in the hours before the Cross. He continued to treat others with the love that He exuded. Why? He treated others with love beyond all measure because God/Jesus/Holy Spirit are love, and He wanted to model treating others with love for all to see. I'll talk more about the Greatest Commandment later.

During classes for a human resource development degree in the early 1990s, I had the pleasure of being instructed by retired army brigadier general Tommy Smith. Being a new air force second lieutenant, I had very wrong preconceived ideas that all army people, especially general officers, were rough, gruff, profane, rude, crude, and cigar-smoking (even the women!). I also assumed they all grunted and yelled a lot! BG Smith was just the opposite. He was kind, soft-spoken, very humble, and an extremely effective instructor. I remember he even drove a very unassuming (though wicked cool) mid 1970s JEEP pickup. Of course, I was paying a hefty monthly payment for a new truck, so the retro look of the "paid-up" JEEP was very attractive.

I remember his leadership advice as if I was sitting in his class only yesterday. "If you are in a leadership position, or even in any relationship, and you have to win all the time, that means the other person has to lose all the time. After a short period of time, people will not desire to be around you, and you will have lost your ability to lead, or even to maintain normal reciprocal friendships." I have thought of BG Smith's lectures and that specific comment time and time over the course of my leadership experiences.

Let's take a minute to talk about honesty. My assumption is that we all want other people to be honest with us. No human being wants to have someone lie to them. Lies can be the downfall of any relationship and turn the workplace into a devastatingly ugly, festering hotbed of anger, malice, and even hatred. In fact, in one of the many places God speaks about lies in the Bible, He says Satan is the father of lies, and there is no truth in him (John 8:44).

James Hunter expands the definition of honesty from not telling lies to being free from deception in any form. In the *Servant Leader*, the teacher who has taken the name of Simeon teaches that "a lie is any communication with the intent to deceive. Not speaking up or withholding pieces of the truth may be thought of as 'little white lies' and socially acceptable, but they are lies nonetheless."

Earlier in the book, Simeon states that when people are polled, honesty is the top quality most people want from their leader. Mr. Hunter also states, through Simeon, that "honesty is about clarifying expectations for people, holding them accountable, being willing to give the bad news as well as the good news, giving people feedback, being consistent, predictable, and fair. In short, our behavior must be free from deception and dedicated to the truth at all cost" (Hunter, 118–119).

We all want people to be honest with us. Yes, sometimes that honesty hurts, especially if the person is not sensitive in sharing honesty that isn't pleasant for you to hear. But in the end, honesty is absolutely the best policy!

I conclude this chapter about the Golden Rule with an online article by Dr. Travis Bradberry, "10 Habits of Ultra-Likable Leaders." Dr. Bradberry is the coauthor of the popular book *Intelligence 2.0* and cofounder of TalentSmart, a leading provider of emotional intelligence tests and training.

Please let me be very clear. I am *not* advocating that the sole goal of leadership is to be the "most liked." I believe that is a ridiculous philosophy. Effective, mission-focused leadership requires decisions and actions that some people simply are not going to like. Moreover, some people are not going to like the person who has taken an unpopular action or made a tough decision. However, there is tons of evidence that at some level, likability is useful in successful leadership. Also, I like the way Dr. Bradberry breaks the overall idea of likeability down to a list of component factors that look amazingly similar to the characteristics and traits I've written about in this book.

Dr. Bradberry states,

> When I speak to smaller audiences, I often ask them to describe the best and worst leaders

they have ever worked for. People inevitably ignore innate characteristics (intelligence, extraversion, attractiveness, and so on) and instead focus on qualities that are completely under the leader's control, such as approachability, humility and positivity.

These words, and others like them, describe leaders who are skilled in emotional intelligence. TalentSmart researches data from more than a million people that shows that leaders who possess these qualities aren't just highly likeable, they outperform those who don't possess them by a large margin.

I believe most all of these traits implement the Golden Rule or are intimately related to the Golden Rule.

What follows are the ten key behaviors that Dr. Bradberry states that emotionally intelligent leaders engage in that make them so likable.

1. THEY FORM PERSONAL CONNECTIONS

Even in a crowded room, likable leaders make people feel like they're having a one-on-one conversation, as if they're the only person in the room that matters. And for that moment, they are. Likable leaders communicate on a very personal, emotional level. They never forget that there's a flesh-and-blood human being standing in front of them.

2. THEY'RE APPROACHABLE

You know those people who only have time for you if you can do something for them? Likable leaders truly believe that everyone, regardless of rank or ability, is worth their time and attention. They make everyone feel valuable because they believe that everyone *is* valuable.

3. THEY'RE HUMBLE

Few things kill likability as quickly as arrogance. Likable leaders don't act as though they're better than you because they don't think that they're better than you. Rather than being a source of prestige, they see their leadership positions as bringing them additional accountability for serving those who follow them.

4. THEY'RE POSITIVE

Likeable leaders always maintain a positive outlook, and this shows in how they describe things. They don't have to give a presentation to the board of directors; they get to share their vision and ideas with the board. They don't have to go on a plant tour; they get to meet and visit with the people who make their company's products. They don't even have to diet; they get to experience the benefits of eating healthfully. Even in undeniably negative situations, likable leaders emanate an enthusiastic hope for the future, a confidence that they can help make tomorrow better than today.

5. THEY'RE EVEN-KEELED

When it comes to their own accomplishments and failures, likable leaders take things in stride. They don't toot their own horns. Nor do they get rattled when they make a big mistake. They savor success without letting it go to their heads, and they readily acknowledge failure without getting mired in it. They learn from both and move on.

6. THEY'RE GENEROUS

We've all worked for someone who constantly holds something back, whether it's knowledge or resources. They act as if they're afraid you'll outshine them if they give you access to everything you need to do your job. Likable leaders are unfailingly generous with whom they know, what they know, and the resources they have access to. They want you to do well more than anything else because they understand that this is their job as a leader and because they're confident enough to never worry that your success might make them look bad. In fact, they believe that your success is their success.

7. THEY DEMONSTRATE INTEGRITY

Likable leaders inspire trust and admiration through their actions, not just their words. Many leaders say that integrity is important to them, but likable leaders walk their talk by demonstrating integrity every day. Even a leader who oozes charm won't be likable if that charm isn't backed by a solid foundation of integrity.

8. THEY READ PEOPLE LIKE A BOOK

Likable leaders know how to read people as unspoken communication is often more important than the words people say. They note facial expressions, body language, and tone of voice in order to understand what's really going on with their people. In other words, they have high social awareness, which is a critical skill.

9. THEY APPRECIATE POTENTIAL

Robert Brault said, "Charisma is not so much getting people to like you as getting people to like themselves when you're around." Likable leaders not only see the best in their people, but they also make sure that everyone else sees it, too. They draw out people's talents so that everyone is bettering themselves and the work at hand.

10. THEY HAVE SUBSTANCE

Daniel Quinn said, "Charisma only wins people's attention. Once you have their attention, you have to have something to tell them." Likable leaders understand that their knowledge and expertise are critical to the success of everyone who follows them. Therefore, they regularly connect with people to share their substance (as opposed to superficial small talk). Likable leaders don't puff themselves up or pretend to be something they're not because they don't have to. They have substance, and they share it with their people.

Likability isn't a birthright; it results from acquirable skills that are crucial to your professional success. And just like any other professional skills, you can study the people who have them, copy what works, and adapt them to your own style. Try these ten strategies and watch your likability soar.

I was blessed to have the opportunity to discuss the theories contained in this book with a great friend. He is an Air Force Medical Service Corps officer who is brilliant in information technology and has an unlimited future in IT and leadership in general, both in the air force and beyond when he retires. He perfectly summed up Dr. Bradberry's thoughts on approachability, humility, and positivity by saying, "People will not remember the tons of wins or accomplishments while working under you as a leader, but they will remember how you treated them. People will always remember a leader, or a person, based on the leader's actions toward them, the leader's compassion for them, and their genuineness. Knowing how the leader responded to his or her people and whether or not the leader made the people feel like they were cared for will go a long way in their memories."

Just as no book on leadership is complete without speaking about integrity, no leadership book, especially a Christian leadership book, would be complete without referencing the incredible body of leadership work by Dr. John Maxwell. Dr. Maxwell is the leading author on leadership in the world. He is also a former preacher, so his focus on people is very representative of someone who has practiced the Golden Rule for many, many years. He has developed hundreds of leadership principles during his wildly successful career. I very much like Dr. Maxwell's "Elevator Principle." In his book *Winning with People*, he describes the Elevator Principle. The Elevator Principle preaches that we can lift people up in our relationships, or we can take them down in our relationships. We must be proactive and lift people up! He quotes a friend of his as saying, "'The world is starving for appreciation. It is hungry for compliments. But somebody must start the ball rolling by speaking first and saying a nice thing to his companion.'"

Dr. Maxwell writes about a friend who started a club called the Compliment Club in a class the friend was teaching. The requirement was to sincerely compliment three people each day for some trait they exhibited, some accomplishment they succeeded in, or even if they looked particularly nice that day. In the original thirty-day experiment, students had to write essays on the difference in the attitude in which they perceived in the people around them and their own attitudes about themselves. As you might imagine, those who sincerely sought out ways to compliment people, and followed up with a thoughtful comment found they were more positive in their overall outlook (Maxwell, 47).

Since I first read *Winning with People* in 2011, I've tried to implement this practice of complimenting several people a day. Of course, there are days where I'm busy or I'm preoccupied with something, and I don't succeed in my goal of complimenting. However, I always appreciate the good feeling that comes when I do remember to sincerely compliment people for various reasons.

In summary for this chapter, practicing what Christ taught in the Golden Rule is not merely about being likable. It is simply remembering that there is an extremely valuable human being in every conversation and every situation, and it's the other person! If we as leaders and fellow humans can look at that other person and remember that they would appreciate being treated as we would appreciate being treated, our daily lives will no doubt become more rewarding and fulfilling. All of us long to be treated with respect, kindness, compassion, and dignity. We all want to feel like we are valued and that our contributions make a difference to the mission of our family or the organization that we work for. We should be kind to others in every way at every opportunity, but remember, that doesn't mean as leaders we should not hold people appropriately accountable in professional and personal relationships.

CHAPTER 11
SLIP SLUGGING AWAY AND THE POWER OF CHOICE

A man doesn't have to look like Dwayne "The Rock" Johnson, Brad Pitt, or Adam Levine to be a great leader. Women, you don't need to look like Jessica Alba or Kate Upton or whatever woman is getting the most magazine covers to be a great leader. A person doesn't need to play football like Tom Brady, play basketball like LeBron James, or be built like John Cena to have authority and influence on others. Anybody can become a great leader regardless of natural personality, whether an extrovert or introvert, and regardless of his or her position. You don't even need to kill a giant with a slingshot like David from the Bible! *Anybody* can become a great leader if he or she simply chooses to put in the effort to be a great leader.

In addition to basketball, I also played football in high school and was blessed to have an inspiring coach. Mr. Don Knock was about six feet two inches tall and built like a brick wall. Even though our team had several very muscular football players (present company excluded), no one was as big as Coach Knock, or matched his intensity! And he knew a lot about football. He had been with Oakland Raiders for a period of time in the early 1980s. He was an amazingly motivational coach and an awesome person.

Coach Knock was also very in tune with the mental aspect of athletic competition. He was on the cutting edge of coaches who treated the mental aspect of learning the game and preparing for competition as important as physical preparation. In fact, he instituted the practice of meditation and relaxation before games. We would all lie on the floor of an empty classroom or the locker room before a game, close our eyes, and begin a meditation routine. Coach Knock would put on a music tape (what I learned later was Baroque music) and lead us through a mental process that consisted of imagining a bright light within us and consuming us. We were to imagine the bright light starting at our heads and expanding from there down to our necks and out to our shoulders, arms, torso, and legs. As the light slowly illuminated through our bodies, we were to imagine that it enlivened, expanded, and forced out impurities and negative energy. The positive beam of energy brought clarity, purity, and power to our bodies and our minds. After we got through the initial suspiciousness about the usefulness of the practice of meditation, and the teenage immature giggling and overall messing around while lying on the floor with fifty-nine other teenage boys, we began to see real results. We were more focused at kick-off and started games more relaxed and more determined. Our energy level going into games was higher and stamina was greater. Over the course of those years under Coach Knock's leadership, the team won two state championships and several conference championships. It's hard to argue with that kind of success!

In addition to the relaxation meditation, Coach Knock used to tell us something that is engrained in my psyche like the stamp of Lincoln on a bright and shiny penny. During the relaxation meditation, and most every day throughout the season, Coach Knock used to impress upon us this mantra: "Your greatest power in life is your power to choose." It is profound in its simplicity, yet that type of thinking can move a mountain the size of Mt. Everest in its application. We can choose how we live our lives! In America and other free nations, we can actually choose the course of our lives! We can go to the college we want (within some logical constraints), we can date or marry whom we want, we can do whatever job we want, and we can *choose* to become great leaders! I've often repeated Coach Knock's words of wisdom to the young men and women I was fortunate enough to lead over the course of my career.

I'm not sure if Coach Knock ever read *Man's Search for Meaning*, but many of his philosophies were very similar to those advanced in the book written by Dr. Viktor E. Frankl. Dr. Frankl was a Jewish psychiatrist imprisoned at the infamous Nazi death camp Auschwitz during WWII. Dr. Frankl's experiences and thoughts about a concentration camp existence are incredibly insightful as a survivor but even more introspective because of his mental health expertise. I'll quote a few passages from his book in which he talks about his findings regarding people's power to choose.

> In attempting this psychological presentation and a psychological explanation of the typical characteristics of a concentration camp inmate, I may give the impression that the human being is completely and unavoidably influenced by his surroundings. (In this case the surroundings being the unique structure of camp life, which forced the prisoner to conform his conduct to a set pattern.) But what about human liberty? Is there no spiritual freedom in regard to behavior and *reaction* to any given surroundings? Is that

theory true which would have us believe that man is no more than a product of many conditional and environmental factors—be they of a biological, psychological or sociological nature? Is man but an accidental product of these? Most important, do the prisoner's reactions to the singular world of the concentration camp prove that man cannot escape the influences of his surroundings? Does man have no choice of action in the face of such circumstances?

We can answer these questions from experience as well as on principle. The experiences of camp life show that man *does* have a choice of action. There were enough examples, often of a heroic nature, which proved that apathy could be overcome, irrationality suppressed. Man *can* preserve a vestige of spiritual freedom, of independence of mind, even in such terrible conditions of psychic and physical stress.

We who lived in concentration camps can remember the men who walked through the huts comforting others, giving away their last piece of bread. They may have been few in number, but they offer sufficient proof that everything can be taken from a man but one thing: the last of the human freedoms—to choose one's attitude in any given set of circumstances, to choose one's own way.

And there were always choices to make. Every day, every hour offered the opportunity to make a decision, a decision which determined whether you would or would not submit

to those powers which threatened to rob you of
your very self, your inner freedom; which determined whether or not you would become the
plaything of circumstance, renouncing freedom
and dignity to become molded into the form of
a typical inmate." (Frankl, 66)

Please read this line again and let it soak deep into your
brain: "everything can be taken from a man but one thing: the
last of the human freedoms—to choose one's attitude in any
given set of circumstances, to choose one's own way." Again,
I *never* want to minimize the gut-wrenching hardships that
many of us have been through; only we can know the internal
pain of devastating events that have happened in our lives. I
would never say that we can wave the magic wand of positive
thinking over a situation, and we will all skip away happy as
larks. However, history has provided us with millions of examples from Jesus Christ to Dr. Frankl to Commander Jeremiah
Denton and to Rocky Bleier that prove that our responses to
the devastating events are where the rubber really meets the
road. Our response to hard times is where we as people, and
as leaders, can choose to pick ourselves up, dust off our pants,
and get back in the ring.

Another one of my Vietnam POW heroes is air force colonel (retired) Lee Ellis. Colonel Ellis was a pilot who was shot
down over North Vietnam in 1967 and spent the next five
years as a POW. He served in that capacity with honor, integrity, character, and perseverance. His friends and fellow POWs
included many of the heroes that I've already mentioned.
Colonel Ellis also struggled side by side with lesser-known but
equally strong, courageous, and humble men such as an officer
and gentleman I had the blessing of meeting and becoming

friends with during the early 2000s in San Antonio, retired air force Colonel Art Burer.

Colonel Burer served and suffered right alongside some of the better-known Hanoi Hilton POWs for over five years. He came home to San Antonio and quietly resumed his life as a husband and father and continued his air force career. He had already retired as a full colonel by the time I met him in 2003. He had a huge impact in his local community and church. He was always very willing to share his POW experiences and how he felt Jesus Christ had carried him through that indescribable ordeal.

Colonel Lee Ellis, however, upon returning from captivity, and after resuming a fulfilling and very successful air force career, became a professional leadership consultant where he assessed, coached, and trained a myriad of professional men and women. His clients include Fortune 500 companies and top leaders in health care, entrepreneurs and entertainers, politicians, plant supervisors, and pastors. Colonel Ellis writes in his book, *Leading with Honor*, that remaining positive about their country, families, and fellow captives was one of the primary ways in which they could survive. He lists three insights and questions to help us reflect on our attitudes of being positive.

1. Engage adversity with a positive attitude: How do we respond when life is not fair? How could we engage in challenges more effectively?
2. Manage your emotions as if they're contagious because they are: What situations have you observed where your negative emotions affected others? How could you handle your negative emotions more productively? Where can we start?
3. Engage change with a plan: Do you intentionally develop plans for dealing with change? (Ellis, 45)

One of my favorite General Patton quotes is, "When you hit bottom, bounce back as high and fast as possible!" Patton went on to say, "Remember when you are standing on two feet you can only kick with one foot. When you are flat on your back you can kick with two feet" (Williamson, 140)! General Patton, Coach Knock, and Colonel Ellis were all saying that when you are at your lowest, that's when you have the opportunity to fight back with your utmost vigor and bounce back higher than you were before the fall. Remember, our greatest power in life is our power to choose!

George Washington Carver has a beautiful quote about what he feels is the essence of humanity; I have to agree with him. "Be kind to others. How far you go in life depends upon your being tender with the young, compassionate with the aged, sympathetic with the striving, tolerant of the weak and the strong. Because someday in your life, you will have been all of these."

Attachment 1 is a summary of the leadership traits I've covered in this book. Make a copy of the leadership traits and pin it to your office wall or cubicle cork board at work. When things are crazy at work, simple look at the leadership traits I've written about, take a step back, and concentrate on what is most important…you being a great leader…at work and at home.

Attachment 2 is a poem both my USAFA roommate of three years, Mike Wollet, and I enjoyed. Mike had memorized it forward and backward. *The Man in the Glass* is a wonderful poem about living a life of character and integrity and being able to look back with pride at the end of a long and well-lived life.

I also want to let the readers know about an incredible generation of Americans who serve this nation and its citizens with selflessness and dedication that rivals any that America has ever seen, and that's the current generation of young Americans who are entering the military to fight the global war on terrorism. You've read about my heroes in this book, many of them from the traditional "Greatest Generation" of WWII and Korea and even into Vietnam. But I'll tell you that *every* generation of American military men and women is the greatest generation. While it's unclear if former British prime minister Tony Blair, or an unknown Internet contributor first spoke this quote, it is one of the most beautiful and most honoring ways to remember of some of the greatest people ever born: "Only two defining forces have ever offered to die for you: 1. Jesus Christ, 2. The American GI. One died for your soul, the other for your freedom."

I love our WWI and WWII veterans for their toughness and ability to withstand severe hardships during the wars with mind-numbing battles and long family separations. I love our Korean War veterans, many of whom were also WWII veterans, for their willingness to go fight an enemy that didn't appear to pose an immediate threat to America. I love our Vietnam veterans who went and fought an unpopular war for war naive politicians. Our Vietnam veterans were younger than America's fighting men and women had ever been, yet went and did their jobs to the best of their ability despite their own American brothers and sisters at home who sometimes despised them for answering their nation's call. America (not just the government, but the people also) still owe our Vietnam veterans a huge apology for how they treated our heroes during and after the conflict. We as a country owe them a huge amount of appreciation for what they did to defend those who weren't able to defend themselves.

I love our Desert Shield/Desert Storm veterans for willingly picking up the torch of freedom from their predecessors and taking the fight to Saddam Hussein and blocking his aggression. This was the first American war fought by a 100 percent volunteer force, and they did an incredible job. And I love our post-9/11 heroes. Many of them joined the military after 9/11 out of a sense of patriotism that drove them to go fight terrorists wherever they might be. They knew they would actually go fight when they joined. They knew they would fight and possibly die at the hands of a ruthless enemy who relied on cowardly tactics such as suicide bombers and the heavy use of improvised explosive devices.

I had the opportunity and blessing of deploying to Kandahar Air Base, Afghanistan, from late 2010 to mid-2011. I worked in the Contingency Aeromedical Staging Facility, located in a tent just off the flight-line. Our job was to orchestrate aeromedical evacuation of recently wounded soldiers, sailors, airmen, and marines to higher levels of medical care at Bagram Air Base in northern Afghanistan and Ramstein Air Base in Germany. Daily we helped prepare and then transport our young wounded warriors to the waiting aircraft on the flight-line. Daily we moved severely wounded heroes, many of them fresh amputees (often multiple limb amputees) to the aircraft. Of the dozens and dozens of amputees that we had the privilege of helping, not a single one was basking in their sorrows. Conversely, they were very disappointed to be leaving their buddies behind. They were determined to get home, recover, and get back to their buddies and the global war on terrorism. They were selfless, courageous, and awe-inspiring. They are equally as great as of any generation of American fighting men and women as there has ever been. I'm proud to have been able to help them in some small way. These young men and women are the warriors of today and national leaders of tomorrow. America will be in good hands if these young men and women enter into roles of government and public service.

I'll close this book with a quote from Russell Crowe as General Maximus Decimus Merius from the popular movie *Gladiator*. The quote is short but one of the most brilliant, profound, and insightful string of words ever spoken: "Brothers, what we do in life echoes in eternity." General Maximus said these words to his soldiers before they entered a bloody battle on behalf of Emperor Marcus Aurelius. I say these same words to you as a reminder to think about the leadership and the life legacy you will leave to those you love and those who love you as a family member, friend, or coworker. I implore you to use your power to choose to be a transformational leader and choose to treat others as you would like to be treated. I beg you to love your fellow person as Jesus, the Son of God, instructs in the Greatest Commandant, quoted in the book of Matthew: [36]"Teacher, which *is* the great commandment in the law?" [37]Jesus said to him, "'You shall love the LORD your God with all your heart, with all your soul, and with all your mind.' [38]This is *the* first and great commandment. [39]And *the* second *is* like it: 'You shall love your neighbor as yourself.' [40]On these two commandments hang all the Law and the Prophets." (Matthew 22:36–40).

Please hear the words of this slug: Please choose to be a great leader; please choose to be a great parent, spouse, son, or daughter; and please choose to love others the way God, through His Son Christ Jesus, loves us. Please pray for America, its government leadership, and its people. Pray that we as a nation recognize and honor God for that is the only way America can survive, thrive, and remain the greatest nation on earth. Thank you. God bless you.

ATTACHMENT 1
LEADERSHIP SECRETS OF A SLUG

1. Integrity

2. Courage over Fear

3. Humbleness

4. Preparedness/Hard Work

5. Patience

6. Communication/Active Listening

7. Situational Awareness/Attention to Detail

8. The Golden Rule

9. The Power to Choose Success

ATTACHMENT 2
THE MAN IN THE GLASS

When you get what you want in your struggle for self and the world makes you king for a day, just go to the mirror and look at yourself, and see what that man has to say.

For it isn't your father or mother or wife whose judgment upon you must pass; the fellow whose verdict counts most in your life is the one staring back from the glass.

He's the fellow to please; never mind all the rest. For he's with you clear up to the end, and you've passed the most dangerous, difficult test if the man in the glass is your friend.

You may be like Jack Horner and "chisel" a plum, and think you're a wonderful guy, but the man in the glass says you're only a bum if you can't look him straight in the eye.

You may fool the whole world down the pathway of years. And get pats on the back as you pass, but your final reward will be the heartaches and tears if you've cheated the man in the glass.

Peter Dale Wimbrow Sr.

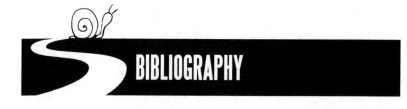

BIBLIOGRAPHY

American Patriot: The Life and Wars of Colonel Bud Day. Robert Coram. Back Bay Books. New York. 2007.

"Become a Stronger Leader by Asking Yourself These Three Questions." Patrick Allen. http://news.monster.com/a/lifestyle/become-a-stronger-leader-by-asking-yourself-these-three-questions. 28 May 15.

Chris Kyle, America Sniper: The Autobiography of the Most Lethal Sniper in U.S. Military History. Chris Kyle, Scott McEwen, and Jim DeFelice. Harper Collins Publishers. New York. 2012.

Conversations with Major Dick Winters. Cole C. Kingseed, The Berkley Publishing Group, New York. 2014.

"Former Cab Driver Helps Liberate WWII France." Michael Lee Stallard. http://www.michaelleestallard.com/former-cab-driver-helps-liberate-wwii-france. *Fox News*, 30 June 15.

Hammer-Proof: A Positive Guide to Values-Based Leadership. Jeffrey Zink. Peak Press. Colorado Springs, CO. 2007.

Jump up to: Badger, Emily (March 7, 2011). "Slugging—The People's Transit." Miller-McCune. Retrieved March 7, 2011.

Jump up to: a b Clarke, Rachel (October 15, 2003). "'Slugging' to avoid Washington slog." *BBC News*. Retrieved March 7, 2011.

Jump up to: "Etiquette and Rules of Slug Lines." Retrieved March 7, 2011. http://www.virginiadot.org/travel/how-virginians-slug-more.asp.

Leading with Honor, Leadership Lessons from the Hanoi Hilton, Lee Ellis. Freedom Star Media, USA, 2012.

Lessons Learned from Colin Powell. JD. Retrieved Oct. 28, 2014. http://sourcesofinsight/lessons-learned-from-colin-powell/.

Lone Survivor. Marcus Luttrell. Little, Brown and Company. New York, Boston, London. 2007.

Man's Search for Meaning. Viktor E. Frankl. Beacon Press. Boston. USA. 1992.

Marine! The Life of Chesty Puller. Burke Davis. Bantam Books. New York. 1962.

"Patience in Leadership: More Discipline than Virtue. Gwyn Teatro. Retrieved November 25, 2015. https://gwynteatro.

wordpress.com/2012/02/19/patience-in-leadership-more-discipline-than-virtue.

Patton's Principles. Porter B. Williamson, Management Systems Consultants. Tucson, Arizona. 1979.

Seal of Honor: Operation Red Wings and the Life of Lt. Michael P. Murphy, USN. Gary Williams. Naval Institute Press. Annapolis, MD. 2010.

"Spurs Culture Creates Competitive Advantage." Michael Lee Stallard. http://www.foxbusiness.com/business-leaders/2015/02/25/nbas-spurs-culture-creates-competitive-advantage/#.VW72JDN3m3A.email. February 25, 2015.

The Holy Bible, New King James Version. Thomas Nelson, Inc. Nashville. 1997.

The Leadership Lessons of Jesus: A Timeless Model for Today's Leaders. Bob Briner and Ray Pritchard. B&H Publishing Group. Nashville. 1997, 1998. Updated and republished, 2008.

The Servant: A Simple Story about the True Essence of Leadership. James C. Hunter. Crown Business. New York. 1998.

To Hell and Back. Audi Murphy. Picodor. New York. 1949.

When Hell was in Session. Jeremiah Denton, Jr. Traditional Press. 1982,

Winning with People. John Maxwell. Nelson Business, a Division of Thomas Nelson. Nashville. 2004.

"10 Habits of Ultra-Likable Leaders." Dr. Travis Bradberry. https://linkedin.com/pulse/essential-habits-ultra-likable-leaders-dr-travis-bradberry. July 6, 2015.

"20 Dozen Tips for Better Communication and Leadership Skills." Judith Zaffirini, PhD. Zaffirini Communications. Laredo, TX. 1998.

If you would like to contact Dana, please email him at LeadershipSecretsofaSlug@hotmail.com

Printed in the United States
By Bookmasters